LOOSE
ME A
L
G

Joshua Olumoye

Cover design by: JOO

Email: harmonyheavenlychurch@gmail.com

Phone: +1 7344474400

Table of Contents

DEDICATION 1

INTRODUCTION..3

CHAPTER 1 6

CHAPTER 2..14

CHAPTER 3..20

CHAPTER 4..24

CHAPTER 5..31

CHAPTER 6..37

CHAPTER 7..41

CHAPTER 8..45

CHAPTER 9..49

CHAPTER 10..59

CHAPTER 11..65

CHAPTER 12..73

CHAPTER 13..87

DEDICATION

This book is dedicated to God the Father, God the Son, and God the Holy Spirit.

ACKNOWLEDGEMENTS

I hereby use this page to acknowledge all the people whom God have use to prepare me for the ministry.

I acknowledge all the men of God whom God uses to pray for me day and night, I pray your labor of love will never be in vain. Also, I thank my family and loved one for their prayer and support.

Finally, I acknowledge the God Almighty whom through the Holy Spirit keep and guide me into all things.

INTRODUCTION

LOOSE ME AND LET ME GO

John 11:39-44

39 Jesus said, Take ye away the stone. Martha, the sister of him that was dead, saith unto him, Lord, by this time he stinketh: for he hath been dead four days.

40 Jesus saith unto her, Said I not unto thee, that, if thou wouldest believe, thou shouldest see the glory of God?

41 Then they took away the stone from the place where the dead was laid. And Jesus lifted up his eyes, and said, Father, I thank thee that thou hast heard me.

42 And I knew that thou hearest me always: but because of the people which stand by I said it, that they may believe that thou hast sent me.

43 And when he thus had spoken, he cried with a loud voice, Lazarus, come forth.

44 And he that was dead came forth, bound hand and foot with graveclothes: and his face was bound about with a napkin. Jesus saith unto them, Loose him, and let him go.

Loose him and let him go, commanded Yeshua to the onlookers after Lazarus came out of the grave.

But today this commandment is written for us, in every area we are being bounded we are to command the devil to lose us and let us go.

To lose is to set free or release from bondage. Yeshua is the only one that can set you free.

Yeshua can bind and can loose and can give power to bind and to lose to whom he wants.

Matthew 16:19

19 And I will give unto thee the keys of the kingdom of heaven: and whatsoever thou shalt bind on earth shall be bound in heaven: and whatsoever thou shalt loose on earth shall be loosed in heaven.

Satan can bind but he cannot set free, in fact there is no loosen in his power, his mission is to take you to hell where he belongs.

The entire human race is bound by Satan through Adam disobedience.

Romans 5:12

12 Wherefore, as by one man sin entered into the world, and death by sin; and so death passed upon all men, for that all have sinned:

And through Yeshua's obedience we are made righteous and set free.

Romans 5:19

19 For as by one man's disobedience many were made sinners, so by the obedience of one shall many be made righteous.

We all need to be loosed, we all need to be set free to make it to heaven and for this to be made possible a price must be paid to legally free us from this bondage and Yeshua came from the father to pay this price with his blood.

The blood of Yeshua paid the price and at the same time appease God on our behalf.

Hebrews 9:22

22 And almost all things are by the law purged with blood; and without shedding of blood is no remission.

Both Satan and Yeshua have a clear mission, Satan came to kill you eternally and Yeshua came to give you eternal life.

John 10:10

10 The thief cometh not, but for to steal, and to kill, and to destroy: I am come that they might have life, and that they might have it more abundantly.

Yeshua has come to set us free from every form of bondages, from every form of prison and cages. And not just set us free but to set us free indeed.

John 8:36

36 If the Son therefore shall make you free, ye shall be free indeed.

Your knowledge of the truth of God will set you free and this book will reveal some truth that will set you free in the name of Yeshua.

John 8:32

32 And ye shall know the truth, and the truth shall make you free.

CHAPTER 1

LIFE AND DEATH

Life and death are very close, it just a thin line between them. They are so close that they both live in the same tongue.

Proverbs 18:21

21 Death and life are in the power of the tongue: and they that love it shall eat the fruit thereof.

The tree of life and death were both present with Adam and Eve in the garden of Eden.

The tree of death was in the garden.

Genesis 2:17

17 But of the tree of the knowledge of good and evil, thou shalt not eat of it: for in the day that thou eatest thereof thou shalt surely die.

Also, the tree of life was there too.

Genesis 3:22

22 And the Lord God said, Behold, the man is become as one of us, to know good and evil: and now, lest he put forth his hand, and take also of the tree of life, and eat, and live forever:

Spiritually the thin line between life and death is choice.

Deuteronomy 30:19

19 I call heaven and earth to record this day against you, that I have set before you life and death, blessing and cursing: therefore choose life, that both thou and thy seed may live:

God gave men freedom to choose. Like in the garden of Eden, there is always life and death and there is always good and evil, with pros and cons. But he will always advise you to choose right so you can live.

Adam and Eve choses death and through them death reign in our lives.

Romans 5:12

12 Wherefore, as by one man sin entered into the world, and death by sin; and so death passed upon all men, for that all have sinned:

The same way the Israelites regardless of all the deliverance and miracles of God upon their live, they chose death because of pleasures of life.

After the death of Joshua, there arose a new generation in Israel, and they turn to another god and God gave them up. Though in his love God keep delivering them to prove them but they keep going back to sin.

Judges 2:10-21

10 And also all that generation were gathered unto their fathers: and there arose another generation after them, which knew not the Lord, nor yet the works which he had done for Israel.

11 And the children of Israel did evil in the sight of the Lord, and served Baalim:

12 And they forsook the Lord God of their fathers, which brought them out of the land of Egypt, and followed other gods, of the gods of the people that were round about them, and bowed themselves unto them, and provoked the Lord to anger.

13 And they forsook the Lord, and served Baal and Ashtaroth.

14 And the anger of the Lord was hot against Israel, and he delivered them into the hands of spoilers that spoiled them, and he sold them into the hands of their enemies round about, so that they could not any longer stand before their enemies.

15 Whithersoever they went out, the hand of the Lord was against them for evil, as the Lord had said, and as the Lord had sworn unto them: and they were greatly distressed.

16 Nevertheless the Lord raised up judges, which delivered them out of the hand of those that spoiled them.

17 And yet they would not hearken unto their judges, but they went a whoring after other gods, and bowed themselves unto them: they turned quickly out of the way which their fathers walked in, obeying the commandments of the Lord; but they did not so.

18 And when the Lord raised them up judges, then the Lord was with the judge, and delivered them out of the hand of their enemies all the days of the judge: for it repented the Lord because of their groanings by reason of them that oppressed them and vexed them.

19 And it came to pass, when the judge was dead, that they returned, and corrupted themselves more than their fathers, in following other gods to serve them, and to bow down unto them; they ceased not from their own doings, nor from their stubborn way.

20 And the anger of the Lord was hot against Israel; and he said, Because that this people hath transgressed my covenant which I commanded their fathers, and have not hearkened unto my voice;

21 I also will not henceforth drive out any from before them of the nations which Joshua left when he died:

GOD DID ALL HE COULD TO KEEP THEM

God does not want the Israelites to go the way of the heathen, but they will not listen.

Ezekiel 20:32-33

32 And that which cometh into your mind shall not be at all, that ye say, We will be as the heathen, as the families of the countries, to serve wood and stone.

33 As I live, saith the Lord God, surely with a mighty hand, and with a stretched out arm, and with fury poured out, will I rule over you:

He said I have no pleasure in your death, why do you want to die?

Ezekiel 33:11

11 Say unto them, As I live, saith the Lord God, I have no pleasure in the death of the wicked; but that the wicked turn from his way and live: turn ye, turn ye from your evil ways; for why will ye die, O house of Israel?

But they refuse and he gave them up.

Romans 1:21-24

21 Because that, when they knew God, they glorified him not as God, neither were thankful; but became vain in their imaginations, and their foolish heart was darkened.

22 Professing themselves to be wise, they became fools,

23 And changed the glory of the uncorruptible God into an image made like to corruptible man, and to birds, and fourfooted beasts, and creeping things.

24 Wherefore God also gave them up to uncleanness through the lusts of their own hearts, to dishonour their own bodies between themselves:

Even when Yeshua came the Jews rejected him, it was only few poor among them that received him.

John 1:11-12

11 He came unto his own, and his own received him not.

12 But as many as received him, to them gave he power to become the sons of God, even to them that believe on his name:

After resurrection and ascension, the Jewish Pharisees and the Sadducees killed the gospel, but through Paul the gospel was awaken among the Gentiles, the poor Gentiles embraces it and were empowered to become the sons of God.

It was the Gentiles that kept the gospel, for the Jews there will be no gospel.

The Gentiles were strong today not because they are special but because of the fact that the gospel was preserve in them and the word of Yeshua came to manifest in their lives.

Matthew 21:42-44

42 Jesus saith unto them, Did ye never read in the scriptures, The stone which the builders rejected, the same is become the head of the corner: this is the Lord's doing, and it is marvellous in our eyes?

43 Therefore say I unto you, The kingdom of God shall be taken from you, and given to a nation bringing forth the fruits thereof.

44 And whosoever shall fall on this stone shall be broken: but on whomsoever it shall fall, it will grind him to powder.

Like the Pharisees and the Sadducees, the pagan Gentile rejected Yeshua but not outrightly.

They change the gospel and turn it upside down, killed the true believers and change everything Yeshua to their pagan god son IZEUS (JESUS is IZEUS meaning son of ZEUZ).

Nevertheless, God has achieved his purpose the truth cannot be hidden forever.

LIFE

Life is not when you are living but when you are in Yeshua HaMashiach those who are not in Yeshua HaMashiach are dead.

That is why he says let the dead bury the dead.

Luke 9:59-60

59 And he said unto another, Follow me. But he said, Lord, suffer me first to go and bury my father.

60 Jesus said unto him, Let the dead bury their dead: but go thou and preach the kingdom of God.

And there is life eternal, which is for the believers after this life.

Paul said for me to live is Christ and to die is gain, because when we die, we live forever.

Philippians 1:21

21 For to me to live is Christ, and to die is gain.

As a believer you have cross from death to life.

John 5:24

24 Verily, verily, I say unto you, He that heareth my word, and believeth on him that sent me, hath everlasting life, and shall not come into condemnation; but is passed from death unto life.

And they that do his will have eternal life.

1 John 2:17

17 And the world passeth away, and the lust thereof: but he that doeth the will of God abideth forever.

And if you are dead, physically, or spiritually in him you will live and you will never die, because he is the resurrection and the life.

John 11:25-26

25 Jesus said unto her, I am the resurrection, and the life: he that believeth in me, though he were dead, yet shall he live:

26 And whosoever liveth and believeth in me shall never die. Believest thou this?

DEATH

Death is in three dimensions.

Spiritual death: Life without Yeshua and Holy Spirit

Physical death: Life without soul and spirit

Eternal death: The final state of unbelievers in hell.

Before the death and the resurrection of Yeshua HaMashiach death was so powerful, but at his death, death and graves loses their power over saints and believers.

Matthew 27:50-53

50 Jesus, when he had cried again with a loud voice, yielded up the ghost.

51 And, behold, the veil of the temple was rent in twain from the top to the bottom; and the earth did quake, and the rocks rent;

52 And the graves were opened; and many bodies of the saints which slept arose,

53 And came out of the graves after his resurrection, and went into the holy city, and appeared unto many.

Death cannot hold him.

Acts 2:24

24 Whom God hath raised up, having loosed the pains of death: because it was not possible that he should be holden of it.

By this reason death and grave were challenged.

1 Corinthians 15:54-55

54 So when this corruptible shall have put on incorruption, and this mortal shall have put on immortality, then shall be brought to pass the saying that is written, Death is swallowed up in victory.

55 O death, where is thy sting? O grave, where is thy victory?

GRAVE OR GRAVEYARD AND GRAVEYARD SPIRITS

Graveyard is the place where the dead are buried. It was the throne and house of death until Yeshua took over.

Romans 14:9

9 For to this end Christ both died, and rose, and revived, that he might be Lord both of the dead and living.

The enemies use the spirit death and the spirit of graveyard to fight against strong believers, particularly when they have tried all and they could not get you, they always resort to the spirit of death or graveyard to fight you.

And this spirit in one sentence kills everything in your life, including you in the spirit and turn you into a walking corpse.

But we have victory in Yeshua, because he is the resurrection, and the life. The only power that can counter the grave and death is the power of resurrection.

John 11:25-26

25 Jesus said unto her, I am the resurrection, and the life: he that believeth in me, though he were dead, yet shall he live:

26 And whosoever liveth and believeth in me shall never die. Believest thou this?

He said I will open you grave and give you a new life again.

Ezekiel 37:12-14

12 Therefore prophesy and say unto them, Thus saith the Lord God; Behold, O my people, I will open your graves, and cause you to come up out of your graves, and bring you into the land of Israel.

13 And ye shall know that I am the Lord, when I have opened your graves, O my people, and brought you up out of your graves,

14 And shall put my spirit in you, and ye shall live, and I shall place you in your own land: then shall ye know that I the Lord have spoken it, and performed it, saith the Lord.

He promises to ransom us from the power of the grave and punish the grave.

Hosea 13:14

14 I will ransom them from the power of the grave; I will redeem them from death: O death, I will be thy plagues; O grave, I will be thy destruction: repentance shall be hid from mine eyes.

Graveyard spirits are the spirit of the dead and they are used by the necromancer, wizard, magician, and sorcerers for evil.

Prayers:

Power calling my names from the gates of the grave, be frustrated in the name of Yeshua.

Any house that has been constructed against me in the heavenlies, on the earth, in the waters atomic bomb of the living God locate and destroy them in the name of Yeshua.

My case file in the kingdoms of darkness catch fire and be destroyed in the name of Yeshua.

Every association of witchcrafts with graveyard powers against my life, scatter in the name of Yeshua.

My head where are you being kept come out in the name of Yeshua; you can no longer stay in the graveyard come out in the name of Yeshua.

The cords of battle that tie me and my siblings break off my life in the name of Yeshua.

Battle that tied me and refuse to let me go; Father swallowed them with your fire in the name of Yeshua.

Battles that know me more than I know myself, that is wasting my time Father kill them in the name of Yeshua.

My head come out from among the dead, come out from among the impossibilities, come out from among the strugglers in the name of Yeshua.

CHAPTER 2

POWER TO BIND AND LOOSE

BIND

To bind someone or something is to tie or fasting him tightly with a cord so he cannot move, it can also mean to cage, imprisoned or tie to a secure place.

In the spirit realm you can be bound easily by covenants and that covenants give legal right to the enemies to attack you.

Enemies, based on the covenants can now use, words, curses, spells, fetters, cobwebs, and other form of magic to bind you, control and manipulate you.

Satan is a master binder; Satan has a foundational legal ground on all mankind through the disobedience of Adam. So, everyone must accept Yeshua as your Lord to get out of the lordship of Satan.

LOOSE

To be loose is to be set free or release from bondage. To be untied or unfastened.

Satan and his agent can bind you, but they cannot loose you without the commandment of God. The truth of the matter is that everyone under Satan is bound for hell fire.

YESHUA IS THE ONLY ONE THAT CAN LOOSE IN HEAVEN AND ON EARTH.

Yeshua is the only one that has power both in heave and on earth.

Matthew 28:18

18 And Jesus came and spake unto them, saying, All power is given unto me in heaven and in earth.

He is the only one that is worthy to lose in heaven and on earth.

Revelation 5:2

2 And I saw a strong angel proclaiming with a loud voice, Who is worthy to open the book, and to loose the seals thereof?

Who is worthy? The Lion tribe of Judah is the only one that is worthy to open the book and loose the seal.

Revelation 5:5

5 And one of the elders saith unto me, Weep not: behold, the Lion of the tribe of Judah, the Root of David, hath prevailed to open the book, and to loose the seven seals thereof.

His mission is well stated, TO SET THE CAPTIVE FREE, spiritually, physically, mentally, and emotionally.

Luke 4:18-19

18 The Spirit of the Lord is upon me, because he hath anointed me to preach the gospel to the poor; he hath sent me to heal the brokenhearted, to preach deliverance to the captives, and recovering of sight to the blind, to set at liberty them that are bruised,

19 To preach the acceptable year of the Lord.

This was recorded in the book of Isaiah 700 years before the birth of Yeshua.

Isaiah 61:1-3

1 The Spirit of the Lord God is upon me; because the Lord hath anointed me to preach good tidings unto the meek; he hath sent me to bind up the brokenhearted, to proclaim liberty to the captives, and the opening of the prison to them that are bound;

2 To proclaim the acceptable year of the Lord, and the day of vengeance of our God; to comfort all that mourn;

3 To appoint unto them that mourn in Zion, to give unto them beauty for ashes, the oil of joy for mourning, the garment of praise for the spirit of heaviness; that they might be called trees of righteousness, the planting of the Lord, that he might be glorified.

Yeshua stops at verse 2a because there was no vengeance while he was around but mercy.

But now, after resurrection there is vengeance from God against your enemies (Luke 18:1-8). Now, there is comfort because of the Holy Spirit in us (John 14:16). Now, he gives beauty for ashes, the oil of joy for mourning, the garment of praise for the spirit of heaviness as exchange, that he might be glorified (2 Corinthians 8:9).

IN HIS PRESENCE THERE IS LIBERTY

In the presence of the Lord chains are broken, prisons were opened, blind eyes were opened, the sick were healed, the lame walk, the deaf hears and the dumb speaks. In his presence there is liberty.

2 Corinthians 3:17

17 Now the Lord is that Spirit: and where the Spirit of the Lord is, there is liberty.

The spirit of the Lord came upon Samson, and he was loosed.

Judges 15:14

14 And when he came unto Lehi, the Philistines shouted against him: and the Spirit of the Lord came mightily upon him, and the cords that were upon his arms became as flax that was burnt with fire, and his bands loosed from off his hands.

He sets kings free.

Job 12:18

18 He looseth the bond of kings, and girdeth their loins with a girdle.

He lose those who are appointed to die.

Psalm 102:20

20 To hear the groaning of the prisoner; to loose those that are appointed to death;

He loses the prisoner.

Psalm 146:7

7 Which executeth judgment for the oppressed: which giveth food to the hungry. The Lord looseth the prisoners:

In his presence chain will lose.

Acts 16:26

26 And suddenly there was a great earthquake, so that the foundations of the prison were shaken: and immediately all the doors were opened, and every one's bands were loosed.

He set the deaf and dumb free.

Mark 7:35

35 And straightway his ears were opened, and the string of his tongue was loosed, and he spake plain.

He loses us from infirmities, no matter how long.

Luke 13:12

12 And when Jesus saw her, he called her to him, and said unto her, Woman, thou art loosed from thine infirmity.

His presence stops the heat of fire and lose their bound.

Daniel 3:25

25 He answered and said, Lo, I see four men loose, walking in the midst of the fire, and they have no hurt; and the form of the fourth is like the Son of God.

His anointing breaks yokes and remove burdens.

Isaiah 10:27

27 And it shall come to pass in that day, that his burden shall be taken away from off thy shoulder, and his yoke from off thy neck, and the yoke shall be destroyed because of the anointing.

When we fast, his power comes in and loses our bands and undo our burdens.

Isaiah 58:6

6 Is not this the fast that I have chosen? to loose the bands of wickedness, to undo the heavy burdens, and to let the oppressed go free, and that ye break every yoke?

We need to wake up, clean up and shake off for our redeemer is here to set us free from wherever we have sold.

Isaiah 52:1-3

1 Awake, awake; put on thy strength, O Zion; put on thy beautiful garments, O Jerusalem, the holy city: for henceforth there shall no more come into thee the uncircumcised and the unclean.

2 Shake thyself from the dust; arise, and sit down, O Jerusalem: loose thyself from the bands of thy neck, O captive daughter of Zion.

3 For thus saith the Lord, Ye have sold yourselves for nought; and ye shall be redeemed without money.

HE GAVE US POWER TO BIND AND LOOSE

Binding and loosing are keys of the kingdom of God. No one has the power to bind and loose but Yeshua. He gave us the believers this power.

Matthew 16:19

19 And I will give unto thee the keys of the kingdom of heaven: and whatsoever thou shalt bind on earth shall be bound in heaven: and whatsoever thou shalt loose on earth shall be loosed in heaven.

When he called Lazarus forth, he commanded those who buried him, those who bound him, all the undertakers to lose him and let him go. So, he will command our adversaries to loose us and let us go.

John 11:44

44 And he that was dead came forth, bound hand and foot with graveclothes: and his face was bound about with a napkin. Jesus saith unto them, Loose him, and let him go.

He commanded his disciples to lose a tied colt and no man can stop them, not even the owner. No one can stop him from delivering us.

Luke 19:30-31

30 Saying, Go ye into the village over against you; in the which at your entering ye shall find a colt tied, whereon yet never man sat: loose him, and bring him hither.

31 And if any man ask you, Why do ye loose him? thus shall ye say unto him, Because the Lord hath need of him.

Truly, the owner challenged them, but they said, "The Lord hath need of him".

Luke 19:33-35

33 And as they were loosing the colt, the owners thereof said unto them, Why loose ye the colt?

34 And they said, The Lord hath need of him.

35 And they brought him to Jesus: and they cast their garments upon the colt, and they set Jesus thereon.

The Lord needs us too, so the enemies got to let go.

Prayers:

Satan, hear the word of the Lord, loose me because the Lord hath need of me in the name of Yeshua.

I receive power to bind and loose in the name of Yeshua.

I bind my spirit, soul and body to Yahweh the Father, Yahweh the Son and to Yahweh the Holy Spirit in the name of Yeshua.

I lose my soul from witchcrafts binding, from occultic binding, from familiar spirit binding, and from marine spirit binding in the name of Yeshua.

I lose my soul from universal mind binding machine; I lose my soul from AI control in the name of Yeshua.

CHAPTER 3

TAKE YE AWAY THE STONE
John 11:39-44

39 Jesus said, Take ye away the stone. Martha, the sister of him that was dead, saith unto him, Lord, by this time he stinketh: for he hath been dead four days.

40 Jesus saith unto her, Said I not unto thee, that, if thou wouldest believe, thou shouldest see the glory of God?

41 Then they took away the stone from the place where the dead was laid. And Jesus lifted up his eyes, and said, Father, I thank thee that thou hast heard me.

42 And I knew that thou hearest me always: but because of the people which stand by I said it, that they may believe that thou hast sent me.

43 And when he thus had spoken, he cried with a loud voice, Lazarus, come forth.

44 And he that was dead came forth, bound hand and foot with graveclothes: and his face was bound about with a napkin. Jesus saith unto them, Loose him, and let him go.

The first statement Yeshua made at the tomb of Lazarus was "Take ye away the stone."

TAKE YE AWAY THE STONE

The first commandment given by Yeshua at the tomb of Lazarus was to take away the stone.

Stone represent hinderances to breakthrough, miracles, and deliverances. Whenever the enemies think they finish you they put stone upon you. Whenever a dead person is buried, they put a stone upon him.

The first thing needed on your journey back to life is for the stone to be taken away, without that nothing can be done.

God said in book of Ezekiel "I will open your grave", so I can breathe on you that you may live.

Ezekiel 37:12-14

12 Therefore prophesy and say unto them, Thus saith the Lord God; Behold, O my people, I will open your graves, and cause you to come up out of your graves, and bring you into the land of Israel.

13 And ye shall know that I am the Lord, when I have opened your graves, O my people, and brought you up out of your graves,

14 And shall put my spirit in you, and ye shall live, and I shall place you in your own land: then shall ye know that I the Lord have spoken it, and performed it, saith the Lord.

Hinderances and obstacles must be removed before you can come out of that grave. The snare must be broken before your soul can escape.

Psalm 124:7

7 Our soul is escaped as a bird out of the snare of the fowlers: the snare is broken, and we are escaped.

Before any major breakthrough in our life, major limitations must be removed and this can only be achieved by you be on the side of the Lord, it is the Lord that will do it, but you must be in right standing. He is the breaker; he goes ahead before us and remove limitations.

Micah 2:13

13 The breaker is come up before them: they have broken up, and have passed through the gate, and are gone out by it: and their king shall pass before them, and the Lord on the head of them.

Stones can be sins, covenants, curses, spell and idols and for God to release his power to remove all these stones we must be born again, repent, renounce and forsake our sins.

These sins, covenants and curses might not be directly from us, but from our parents and ancestors, the good news is that they can all be removed by the same process.

Before you continue take these prayers to be born again or for rededication to Yeshua HaMashiach. If you are born again before, say this prayer because Yeshua HaMashiach is the real name of the Son of Yahweh.

Prayers:

Father in the name of Yeshua I confess that I am a sinner and I repent of my sins, and I ask that you forgive me. I confess with my mouth that Yeshua is Lord and I believe in my heart that he died for my sins and that Yahweh raised him from the dead. I declare that I will follow and serve Yeshua from now on and forever in the name of Yeshua. Amen!

Father in the name of Yeshua I renounce ZEUS, I renounce Antichrist, I renounce counterfeit Spirit, I renounce kundalini and I rededicate my life to Yeshua HaMashiach in the name of Yeshua.

Father, I repent of the sins of my parents, the sins of my ancestors. I forgive my parents, my ancestors and anyone that have sin against me, and I believe you will forgive me of all sins in the name of Yeshua.

I break every covenant I have entered into or any covenants anyone has entered into on my behalf in the name of Yeshua.

I break all curses and spells associated with those covenants and I break all curses and spells operating in my life in the name of Yeshua.

I receive blessings for curses, and I break all ungodly soul ties. I bind my soul to Yeshua HaMashiach from henceforth in the name of Yeshua.

NOTE:

Stones or obstacles are not automatically removed after salvation, this is just a necessary and compulsory step to removing them.

After salvation you must continue with God steadfastly in prayer and fasting without ceasing to increase the power of God in you, holy living for Holy Spirit to stay with you and meditating on the word of God for growth. Do deliverance, do bloodline cleansing and do regular warfare prayers.

Do all things necessary to get your complete deliverance.

Prayers:

Owners of evil loads upon my life and destiny carry your load in the name of Yeshua.

Stones upon my life be rolled away in the name of Yeshua.

Graveyard stone and sand upon my pictures be lifted in the name of Yeshua.

Every everlasting gate and doors shut against my life and destiny hear the word of the Lord be lifted because the king of glory is leading me in in the name of Yeshua.

Angel that rolls away the stone from the tomb of Yeshua HaMashiach roll away every stone place upon my life in the name of Yeshua.

I command Yeshua HaMashiach the head corner stone to fall upon any man or woman putting stones upon my life in the name of Yeshua.

I am a burdensome stone; I break in pieces anyone blocking my life with stones in the name of Yeshua (Zechariah 12:3).

CHAPTER 4

BY THIS TIME, HE STINKS
John 11:39-44

39 Jesus said, Take ye away the stone. Martha, the sister of him that was dead, saith unto him, Lord, by this time he stinketh: for he hath been dead four days.

40 Jesus saith unto her, Said I not unto thee, that, if thou wouldest believe, thou shouldest see the glory of God?

41 Then they took away the stone from the place where the dead was laid. And Jesus lifted up his eyes, and said, Father, I thank thee that thou hast heard me.

42 And I knew that thou hearest me always: but because of the people which stand by I said it, that they may believe that thou hast sent me.

43 And when he thus had spoken, he cried with a loud voice, Lazarus, come forth.

44 And he that was dead came forth, bound hand and foot with graveclothes: and his face was bound about with a napkin. Jesus saith unto them, Loose him, and let him go.

BY THIS TIME, HE STINKS

After the commandment by Yeshua to take away the stone,

"Martha, the sister of him that was dead, saith unto him, Lord, by this time he stinketh: for he hath been dead four days".

What was Martha saying? By this time, he stinks. She is saying Lord there is no hope the maggot and worms has started eating him up. He is decayed already.

When all hope is lost then the case is stinking.

At the Red Sea the Israelites were stinking.

By the wall of Jericho, the Israelites were stinking.

On the fourth day the dead body is already stinking, because the magot and worms have started working.

Martha said, Lord there is no hope. Sometimes our case is seeming hopeless but there is no hopeless situation with God. He dealt with all hopeless situation that met him and change them to history and good history for that matter.

FROM HOPELESS SITUATION TO ACCOMPLISHED STATE.

Our God is the God of all flesh there is nothing impossible for him.

Jeremiah 32:27

27 Behold, I am the Lord, the God of all flesh: is there any thing too hard for me?

The God of all flesh visited hopeless Sarah and Sarah had a son when it was impossible for women to have child.

Genesis 18:14

14 Is any thing too hard for the Lord? At the time appointed I will return unto thee, according to the time of life, and Sarah shall have a son.

The dry bones in the book of Ezekiel were hopeless but for the God of all flesh the dry bones lived again.

Ezekiel 37:1-10

1 The hand of the Lord was upon me, and carried me out in the spirit of the Lord, and set me down in the midst of the valley which was full of bones,

2 And caused me to pass by them round about: and, behold, there were very many in the open valley; and, lo, they were very dry.

3 And he said unto me, Son of man, can these bones live? And I answered, O Lord God, thou knowest.

4 Again he said unto me, Prophesy upon these bones, and say unto them, O ye dry bones, hear the word of the Lord.

5 Thus saith the Lord God unto these bones; Behold, I will cause breath to enter into you, and ye shall live:

6 And I will lay sinews upon you, and will bring up flesh upon you, and cover you with skin, and put breath in you, and ye shall live; and ye shall know that I am the Lord.

7 So I prophesied as I was commanded: and as I prophesied, there was a noise, and behold a shaking, and the bones came together, bone to his bone.

8 And when I beheld, lo, the sinews and the flesh came up upon them, and the skin covered them above: but there was no breath in them.

9 Then said he unto me, Prophesy unto the wind, prophesy, son of man, and say to the wind, Thus saith the Lord God; Come from the four winds, O breath, and breathe upon these slain, that they may live.

10 So I prophesied as he commanded me, and the breath came into them, and they lived, and stood up upon their feet, an exceeding great army.

The tree that is cut downs is hopeless but for the smell of the living water they bud again.

Job 14:7-9

7 For there is hope of a tree, if it be cut down, that it will sprout again, and that the tender branch thereof will not cease.

8 Though the root thereof wax old in the earth, and the stock thereof die in the ground;

9 Yet through the scent of water it will bud, and bring forth boughs like a plant.

Your truncated life can be restored again.

Death of four days is hopeless but for the resurrection and the life, the dead lived again.

John 11:25-26

25 Jesus said unto her, I am the resurrection, and the life: he that believeth in me, though he were dead, yet shall he live:

26 And whosoever liveth and believeth in me shall never die. Believest thou this?

Jerusalem beginning was hopeless but for love, God cause her to live.

Ezekiel 16:3-6

3 And say, Thus saith the Lord God unto Jerusalem; Thy birth and thy nativity is of the land of Canaan; thy father was an Amorite, and thy mother an Hittite.

4 And as for thy nativity, in the day thou wast born thy navel was not cut, neither wast thou washed in water to supple thee; thou wast not salted at all, nor swaddled at all.

5 None eye pitied thee, to do any of these unto thee, to have compassion upon thee; but thou wast cast out in the open field, to the lothing of thy person, in the day that thou wast born.

6 And when I passed by thee, and saw thee polluted in thine own blood, I said unto thee when thou wast in thy blood, Live; yea, I said unto thee when thou wast in thy blood, Live.

Shadrach Meshach and Abednego were hopeless but for the Fourth Man they walk freely in the fiery furnace and the fire had no power on them.

Daniel 3:24-27

24 Then Nebuchadnezzar the king was astonished, and rose up in haste, and spake, and said unto his counsellors, Did not we cast three men bound into the midst of the fire? They answered and said unto the king, True, O king.

25 He answered and said, Lo, I see four men loose, walking in the midst of the fire, and they have no hurt; and the form of the fourth is like the Son of God.

26 Then Nebuchadnezzar came near to the mouth of the burning fiery furnace, and spake, and said, Shadrach, Meshach, and Abednego, ye servants of the most high God, come forth, and come hither. Then Shadrach, Meshach, and Abednego, came forth of the midst of the fire.

27 And the princes, governors, and captains, and the king's counsellors, being gathered together, saw these men, upon whose bodies the fire had no power, nor was an hair of their head singed, neither were their coats changed, nor the smell of fire had passed on them.

Daniel at the den of lion is hopeless but for the Lion tribe of Judah, the lion could not harm him because God shut their mouth.

Daniel 6:20-23

20 And when he came to the den, he cried with a lamentable voice unto Daniel: and the king spake and said to Daniel, O Daniel, servant of the living God, is thy God, whom thou servest continually, able to deliver thee from the lions?

21 Then said Daniel unto the king, O king, live for ever.

22 My God hath sent his angel, and hath shut the lions' mouths, that they have not hurt me: forasmuch as before him innocency was found in me; and also before thee, O king, have I done no hurt.

23 Then was the king exceedingly glad for him, and commanded that they should take Daniel up out of the den. So Daniel was taken up out of the den, and no manner of hurt was found upon him, because he believed in his God.

David at the battle against Goliath is hopeless but for the Lord of host, Goliath was defeated.

1 Samuel 17:45-51

45 Then said David to the Philistine, Thou comest to me with a sword, and with a spear, and with a shield: but I come to thee in the name of the Lord of hosts, the God of the armies of Israel, whom thou hast defied.

46 This day will the Lord deliver thee into mine hand; and I will smite thee, and take thine head from thee; and I will give the carcases of the host of the Philistines this day unto the fowls of the air, and to the wild beasts of the earth; that all the earth may know that there is a God in Israel.

47 And all this assembly shall know that the Lord saveth not with sword and spear: for the battle is the Lord's, and he will give you into our hands.

48 And it came to pass, when the Philistine arose, and came, and drew nigh to meet David, that David hastened, and ran toward the army to meet the Philistine.

49 And David put his hand in his bag, and took thence a stone, and slang it, and smote the Philistine in his forehead, that the stone sunk into his forehead; and he fell upon his face to the earth.

50 So David prevailed over the Philistine with a sling and with a stone, and smote the Philistine, and slew him; but there was no sword in the hand of David.

51 Therefore David ran, and stood upon the Philistine, and took his sword, and drew it out of the sheath thereof, and slew him, and cut off his head therewith. And when the Philistines saw their champion was dead, they fled.

The black race is hopeless but for the recognition of Yeshua HaMashiach their identity, they will be restored.

Matthew 23:37-39

37 O Jerusalem, Jerusalem, thou that killest the prophets, and stonest them which are sent unto thee, how often would I have gathered thy children together, even as a hen gathereth her chickens under her wings, and ye would not!

38 Behold, your house is left unto you desolate.

39 For I say unto you, Ye shall not see me henceforth, till ye shall say, Blessed is he that cometh in the name of the Lord.

We say bless is you, Lord.

Psalm 118:26

26 Blessed be he that cometh in the name of the Lord: we have blessed you out of the house of the LORD.

The whole world is hopeless but for the love of God.

John 3:16

16 For God so loved the world, that he gave his only begotten Son, that whosoever believeth in him should not perish, but have everlasting life.

We are hopeless but for mercy.

Lamentations 3:22-23

22 It is of the Lord's mercies that we are not consumed, because his compassions fail not.

23 They are new every morning: great is thy faithfulness.

You might be wondering where and how will this battle end. Where does the ram that substitute Isaac came from?

Genesis 22:13

13 And Abraham lifted up his eyes, and looked, and behold behind him a ram caught in a thicket by his horns: and Abraham went and took the ram, and offered him up for a burnt offering in the stead of his son.

We just don't know how but he will do it. God of all flesh he makes way to escape in hopeless situation.

1 Corinthians 10:13

13 There hath no temptation taken you but such as is common to man: but God is faithful, who will not suffer you to be tempted above that ye are able; but will with the temptation also make a way to escape, that ye may be able to bear it.

How far is your case? Is it stinking. Is all hope lost? Take it to the God of all flesh.

Prayers:

Every stinking situation in my life be reverse by the power of resurrection in the name of Yeshua.

God of all flesh answer your name in my life in the name of Yeshua.

Father, make a way for me now in the name of Yeshua.

CHAPTER 5

BELIEVE AND YOU WILL SEE THE GLORY OF GOD

John 11:39-44

39 Jesus said, Take ye away the stone. Martha, the sister of him that was dead, saith unto him, Lord, by this time he stinketh: for he hath been dead four days.

40 Jesus saith unto her, Said I not unto thee, that, if thou wouldest believe, thou shouldest see the glory of God?

41 Then they took away the stone from the place where the dead was laid. And Jesus lifted up his eyes, and said, Father, I thank thee that thou hast heard me.

42 And I knew that thou hearest me always: but because of the people which stand by I said it, that they may believe that thou hast sent me.

43 And when he thus had spoken, he cried with a loud voice, Lazarus, come forth.

44 And he that was dead came forth, bound hand and foot with graveclothes: and his face was bound about with a napkin. Jesus saith unto them, Loose him, and let him go.

In verse 40 Yeshua said unto Martha "Said I not unto thee, that, if thou wouldest believe, thou shouldest see the glory of God?"

Yeshua had earlier told her in John 11:25-26 that don't be afraid your brother will be brought back to life for I am the resurrection and the life and Martha said I believed, hoping Yeshua was talking about the last day, according to their initial conversation.

John 11:23-24

23 Jesus saith unto her, Thy brother shall rise again.

24 Martha saith unto him, I know that he shall rise again in the resurrection at the last day.

If you believe God, even in the hardest situation you will see the glory of God.

John 11:44

40 Jesus saith unto her, Said I not unto thee, that, if thou wouldest believe, thou shouldest see the glory of God?

When you believe God, you will see his glory. Abraham was the epitome of believe bible calls him the father of faith and our example.

Galatians 3:6-9

6 Even as Abraham believed God, and it was accounted to him for righteousness.

7 Know ye therefore that they which are of faith, the same are the children of Abraham.

8 And the scripture, foreseeing that God would justify the heathen through faith, preached before the gospel unto Abraham, saying, In thee shall all nations be blessed.

9 So then they which be of faith are blessed with faithful Abraham.

God told him to sacrifice Isaac the promised child, he did not hesitate believing God is always good and God at the end supply a lamb to be killed instead of Isaac (Genesis 22:1-18).

BELIEVE

To believe is to have faith in God. Believe for all things are possible to them that believe.

Mark 9:23

23 Jesus said unto him, If thou canst believe, all things are possible to him that believeth.

Stop worrying and just believe there is a mansion in heaven for you, everything you see here in the physical are inferior to the heavenly ones.

John 14:1-2

1 Let not your heart be troubled: ye believe in God, believe also in me.

2 In my Father's house are many mansions: if it were not so, I would have told you. I go to prepare a place for you.

Believe and doubt not, ye shall remove obstacles and mountains.

Matthew 21:21

21 Jesus answered and said unto them, Verily I say unto you, If ye have faith, and doubt not, ye shall not only do this which is done to the fig tree, but also if ye shall say unto this mountain, Be thou removed, and be thou cast into the sea; it shall be done.

We don't have to see it before we believe it but believe it before you see it and that is faith.

Romans 8:24-25

24 For we are saved by hope: but hope that is seen is not hope: for what a man seeth, why doth he yet hope for?

25 But if we hope for that we see not, then do we with patience wait for it.

For faith is the evidence of things not seeing

Hebrews 11:1

1 Now faith is the substance of things hoped for, the evidence of things not seen.

Believe for that is the only way a just man shall live.

Romans 1:17

17 For therein is the righteousness of God revealed from faith to faith: as it is written, The just shall live by faith.

Galatians 3:11

11 But that no man is justified by the law in the sight of God, it is evident: for, The just shall live by faith.

It is the way we walk as a believer.

2 Corinthians 5:7

7 (For we walk by faith, not by sight:)

And we overcome the world by faith.

1 John 5:4

4 For whatsoever is born of God overcometh the world: and this is the victory that overcometh the world, even our faith.

We please God by our faith.

Hebrews 11:6

6 But without faith it is impossible to please him: for he that cometh to God must believe that he is, and that he is a rewarder of them that diligently seek him.

And for the glory of God to be revealed and released in our life we must have faith.

John 11:44

40 Jesus saith unto her, Said I not unto thee, that, if thou wouldest believe, thou shouldest see the glory of God?

GLORY OF GOD

There is glory of men and there is glory of God and what God wanted for us is his glory not our glory.

For we have all come short of his glory because of sins and this glory is back as a believer but we need faith to see it.

Romans 3:23

23 For all have sinned, and come short of the glory of God;

Men's glory is nothing because.

The glory of man can be stolen but the glory of God can never be stolen.

John 10:10

10 The thief cometh not, but for to steal, and to kill, and to destroy: I am come that they might have life, and that they might have it more abundantly.

The glory of men fades away, the glory of God is everlasting.

1 Peter 1:24

24 For all flesh is as grass, and all the glory of man as the flower of grass. The grass withereth, and the flower thereof falleth away:

He came to save us, to deliver us, and to bless us for his glory. He does everything that he might be glorified.

Isaiah 61:1-3

1 The Spirit of the Lord God is upon me; because the Lord hath anointed me to preach good tidings unto the meek; he hath sent me to bind up the brokenhearted, to proclaim liberty to the captives, and the opening of the prison to them that are bound;

2 To proclaim the acceptable year of the Lord, and the day of vengeance of our God; to comfort all that mourn;

3 To appoint unto them that mourn in Zion, to give unto them beauty for ashes, the oil of joy for mourning, the garment of praise for the spirit of heaviness; that they might be called trees of righteousness, the planting of the Lord, that he might be glorified.

The commandment to arise and shine in Isaiah 60 is all because of his glory that is risen upon us and not about ours.

Isaiah 60:1-2

1 Arise, shine; for thy light is come, and the glory of the Lord is risen upon thee.

2 For, behold, the darkness shall cover the earth, and gross darkness the people: but the Lord shall arise upon thee, and his glory shall be seen upon thee.

Moses said, I beseech thee, shew me thy glory.

Exodus 33:18

18 And he said, I beseech thee, shew me thy glory.

As a believer we must not share his glory with ourselves or other gods but give him glory for all things in our life.

Psalm 29:2

2 Give unto the Lord the glory due unto his name; worship the Lord in the beauty of holiness.

For he will not share his glory with anyone.

Isaiah 42:8

8 I am the Lord: that is my name: and my glory will I not give to another, neither my praise to graven images.

Prayers:

I believe Lord show me thy glory in the name of Yeshua.

I believe Lord show me that you are the one with the 3 Hebrew boys in the fire in the name of Yeshua.

I believe Lord show me that you are the alpha and omega in the name of Yeshua.

I believe Lord show me that you are the resurrection and the life in the name of Yeshua.

Father, I believe help my unbelief in the name of Yeshua.

Glory of the living God manifest in my life in the name of Yeshua.

Glory of God the living God upon my life blind my enemies in the name of Yeshua.

CHAPTER 6

THE STONE WAS TAKEN AWAY
John 11:39-44

39 Jesus said, Take ye away the stone. Martha, the sister of him that was dead, saith unto him, Lord, by this time he stinketh: for he hath been dead four days.

40 Jesus saith unto her, Said I not unto thee, that, if thou wouldest believe, thou shouldest see the glory of God?

41 Then they took away the stone from the place where the dead was laid. And Jesus lifted up his eyes, and said, Father, I thank thee that thou hast heard me.

42 And I knew that thou hearest me always: but because of the people which stand by I said it, that they may believe that thou hast sent me.

43 And when he thus had spoken, he cried with a loud voice, Lazarus, come forth.

44 And he that was dead came forth, bound hand and foot with graveclothes: and his face was bound about with a napkin. Jesus saith unto them, Loose him, and let him go.

THE STONE WAS TAKEN AWAY
John 11:41

41 Then they took away the stone from the place where the dead was laid. And Jesus lifted up his eyes, and said, Father, I thank thee that thou hast heard me.

Until the stone was taken away Yeshua did not pray. But the moment the stone was taken away bible says

John 11:41-42

41 Then they took away the stone from the place where the dead was laid. And Jesus lifted up his eyes, and said, Father, I thank thee that thou hast heard me.

42 And I knew that thou hearest me always: but because of the people which stand by I said it, that they may believe that thou hast sent me.

In verse 39 Yeshua told them to take away the stone, which stand as hinderance to the work of God.

Here in verse 41 the stone was taken away by the reason of the one who commanded them.

This implies that the barrier, the hinderances has been removed.

The stone blocking our social, financial, career, physical and our spiritual breakthrough has been removed.

Before Yeshua came, we are separated from God by sins and iniquities just like the stone separated Yeshua from Lazarus.

Isaiah 59:1-4

1 Behold, the Lord's hand is not shortened, that it cannot save; neither his ear heavy, that it cannot hear:

2 But your iniquities have separated between you and your God, and your sins have hid his face from you, that he will not hear.

3 For your hands are defiled with blood, and your fingers with iniquity; your lips have spoken lies, your tongue hath muttered perverseness.

4 None calleth for justice, nor any pleadeth for truth: they trust in vanity, and speak lies; they conceive mischief, and bring forth iniquity.

Today Yeshua our peace and the breaker has broken down that wall of partition between us and God at his resurrection.

Ephesians 2:14

14 For he is our peace, who hath made both one, and hath broken down the middle wall of partition between us;

The moment you give your life to him the wall is removed but you need to fix the legal ground given to Satan by you, your parents and ancestors, also you will have to fight the compulsory fight of temptations.

Yeshua at his resurrection ensured that these walls which is the sins, or stones, that separated us from God was permanently removed, so the Lord send his angel to roll the stone away from his tomb and sat upon it.

Matthew 28:1-6

1 In the end of the sabbath, as it began to dawn toward the first day of the week, came Mary Magdalene and the other Mary to see the sepulchre.

2 And, behold, there was a great earthquake: for the angel of the Lord descended from heaven, and came and rolled back the stone from the door, and sat upon it.

3 His countenance was like lightning, and his raiment white as snow:
4 And for fear of him the keepers did shake, and became as dead men.

5 And the angel answered and said unto the women, Fear not ye: for I know that ye seek Jesus, which was crucified.

6 He is not here: for he is risen, as he said. Come, see the place where the Lord lay.

This stone represents every stone that the devil might place upon you, stone of death, stone of debts, stone of infirmities, stone of poverty, stone of barrenness and whatever stone they choose.

This stone also represents every sin that can hinders us. We need to be reflecting on this and know that the stone has been rolled away.

Prayers:

Father, I pray against every spirit of blockage and barriers operating in my life in the name of Yeshua.

Father, break any barrier that blocks me from being close to you, remove it, Lord! In the name of Yeshua.

I curse out every evil spirit in my life that attempts to hinder my blessings and I command them to leave now in the name of Yeshua.

I rebuke every negative thought and negative word spoken against me and my family that has become hinderances in our life I command you break every off now in the name of Yeshua.

Every wall of Jericho standing between me, and my blessings fall down flat in the name of Yeshua.

Father let every stronghold vanish at the sound of your great name in the name of Yeshua.

Father, raise me up, so that I will overcome mountains and prevail against any blockage, barrier, or hindrance in my life in the name of Yeshua.

CHAPTER 7

YESHUA PRAYED

John 11:39-44

39 Jesus said, Take ye away the stone. Martha, the sister of him that was dead, saith unto him, Lord, by this time he stinketh: for he hath been dead four days.

40 Jesus saith unto her, Said I not unto thee, that, if thou wouldest believe, thou shouldest see the glory of God?

41 Then they took away the stone from the place where the dead was laid. And Jesus lifted up his eyes, and said, Father, I thank thee that thou hast heard me.

42 And I knew that thou hearest me always: but because of the people which stand by I said it, that they may believe that thou hast sent me.

43 And when he thus had spoken, he cried with a loud voice, Lazarus, come forth.

44 And he that was dead came forth, bound hand and foot with graveclothes: and his face was bound about with a napkin. Jesus saith unto them, Loose him, and let him go.

YESHUA PRAYED

After the stone was taken away, Yeshua prayed before calling forth Lazarus.

John 11:41-42

41 Then they took away the stone from the place where the dead was laid. And Jesus lifted up his eyes, and said, Father, I thank thee that thou hast heard me.

42 And I knew that thou hearest me always: but because of the people which stand by I said it, that they may believe that thou hast sent me.

This is showing us the power of praying to the father in the name of Yeshua.

This is showing us humility. He did not say I am God and so I call you forth, but he prayed to the father.

Also, Yeshua shows us the power of prayers, in the any situation we may find ourselves we should pray.

Death and life are in the power of the tongues, we must use our tongue right and we will reap the good fruit from it. If we choose life, we live and if we choose death we die.

Proverbs 18:21

21 Death and life are in the power of the tongue: and they that love it shall eat the fruit thereof.

As Yeshua was praying power of resurrection was activated, life was activated, and Lazarus woke up.

Though death is the final enemy to be destroyed, but power of resurrection has power over death at any moment and at any time.

1 Corinthians 15:26

26 The last enemy that shall be destroyed is death.

This prayer was shorth, but it was all focus on God, the prayer gives all glory to God and God in return release all his glory.

Another short prayer like that in the bible was prayed by Elijah and God in return releases all his glory.

1 Kings 18:36-37

36 And it came to pass at the time of the offering of the evening sacrifice, that Elijah the prophet came near, and said, Lord God of Abraham, Isaac, and of Israel, let it be known this day that thou art God in Israel, and that I am thy servant, and that I have done all these things at thy word.

37 Hear me, O Lord, hear me, that this people may know that thou art the Lord God, and that thou hast turned their heart back again.

And in the next verses the fire fell, and people glorified God.

1 Kings 18:38-39

38 Then the fire of the Lord fell, and consumed the burnt sacrifice, and the wood, and the stones, and the dust, and licked up the water that was in the trench.

39 And when all the people saw it, they fell on their faces: and they said, The Lord, he is the God; the Lord, he is the God.

We must learn and begin to focus our prayer to glorify God, just Yeshua thought us in the Lord's prayer.

Matthew 6:9-13

9 After this manner therefore pray ye: Our Father which art in heaven, Hallowed be thy name.

10 Thy kingdom come, Thy will be done in earth, as it is in heaven.

11 Give us this day our daily bread.

12 And forgive us our debts, as we forgive our debtors.

13 And lead us not into temptation, but deliver us from evil: For thine is the kingdom, and the power, and the glory, for ever. Amen.

Worship and thanking him from the beginning and ended with worship and thanksgiving.

POWER OF RESURRECTION

The power of resurrection was activated while Yeshua was praying. This power does not do anything than to restore back to life or to original state. In this power there is restoration, recovery, reversal, and transformation.

This is the greatest power in heaven and on earth, this power swallow's death in victory and challenge death even before the end time.

1 Corinthians 15:54-55

54 So when this corruptible shall have put on incorruption, and this mortal shall have put on immortality, then shall be brought to pass the saying that is written, Death is swallowed up in victory.

55 O death, where is thy sting? O grave, where is thy victory?

This is the power that raise Yeshua HaMashiach from the dead in the third day and bible says if this power dwells in you it shall raise you up from spiritual or physical death.

Romans 8:11

11 But if the Spirit of him that raised up Jesus from the dead dwell in you, he that raised up Christ from the dead shall also quicken your mortal bodies by his Spirit that dwelleth in you.

Paul so desires this power and he wanted to know more about it and if possible, to attain it.

Philippians 3:10-11

10 That I may know him, and the power of his resurrection, and the fellowship of his sufferings, being made conformable unto his death;

11 If by any means I might attain unto the resurrection of the dead.

It was the power of resurrection that raises Lazarus from the dead.

It was the power of resurrection that raises Jairus daughter.

It was the power of resurrection that opens the eyes of blind Bartimaeus.

It was the power of resurrection that causes the dry bones to live again.

It was the power of resurrection that makes the axe head to swim again.

It was the power of resurrection that raises our Lord Yeshua HaMashiach from the dead.

It is the power of resurrection that can restore to you the years that the locust has eaten.

Prayers:

Holy Ghost come upon my life; power of resurrection overshadows me in the name of Yeshua.

Power of resurrection incubate my life in the name of Yeshua.

Power of resurrection manifest in my dream in the name of Yeshua.

Power of resurrection fall upon my dead virtues in the name of Yeshua.

Power of resurrection swallow the spirit of death assign against me in the name of Yeshua.

CHAPTER 8

LAZARUS, COME FORTH
John 11:39-44

39 Jesus said, Take ye away the stone. Martha, the sister of him that was dead, saith unto him, Lord, by this time he stinketh: for he hath been dead four days.

40 Jesus saith unto her, Said I not unto thee, that, if thou wouldest believe, thou shouldest see the glory of God?

41 Then they took away the stone from the place where the dead was laid. And Jesus lifted up his eyes, and said, Father, I thank thee that thou hast heard me.

42 And I knew that thou hearest me always: but because of the people which stand by I said it, that they may believe that thou hast sent me.

43 And when he thus had spoken, he cried with a loud voice, Lazarus, come forth.

44 And he that was dead came forth, bound hand and foot with graveclothes: and his face was bound about with a napkin. Jesus saith unto them, Loose him, and let him go.

LAZARUS, COME FORTH
John 11:43

43 And when he thus had spoken, he cried with a loud voice, Lazarus, come forth.

After prayers Yeshua called Lazarus forth, there is one important thing in this verse, bible says "he cried with a loud voice."

There are times to pray silently and there are times to speak out and there are times to cry out loudly, and you cry out with a loud voice whenever you are calling.

Calling forth is not an easy task it takes great faith, especially for the believers.

Elijah closed the heaven with just a word, and it was so, but calling forth the rain was more difficult.

1 Kings 17:1

1 And Elijah the Tishbite, who was of the inhabitants of Gilead, said unto Ahab, As the Lord God of Israel liveth, before whom I stand, there shall not be dew nor rain these years, but according to my word.

He prayed earnestly for the rain to come forth, but nothing happens until the seventh time.

1 Kings 18:41-46

41 And Elijah said unto Ahab, Get thee up, eat and drink; for there is a sound of abundance of rain.

42 So Ahab went up to eat and to drink. And Elijah went up to the top of Carmel; and he cast himself down upon the earth, and put his face between his knees,

43 And said to his servant, Go up now, look toward the sea. And he went up, and looked, and said, There is nothing. And he said, Go again seven times.

44 And it came to pass at the seventh time, that he said, Behold, there ariseth a little cloud out of the sea, like a man's hand. And he said, Go up, say unto Ahab, Prepare thy chariot, and get thee down that the rain stop thee not.

45 And it came to pass in the mean while, that the heaven was black with clouds and wind, and there was a great rain. And Ahab rode, and went to Jezreel.

46 And the hand of the Lord was on Elijah; and he girded up his loins, and ran before Ahab to the entrance of Jezreel.

There are lot of things to call forth in our lives, everything stolen, killed, and destroyed must be called back.

The glory of God in our life must be call forth, our original must be called forth, our lost virtues and destiny must be call forth. Whatever is lost must be call forth.

Yeshua called the dead to come forth. You must get to the level of faith of calling things to manifest. Even things that you did not have, and you wanted if it is according to the will of God can be call forth.

Romans 4:17

17 (As it is written, I have made thee a father of many nations,) before him whom he believed, even God, who quickeneth the dead, and calleth those things which be not as though they were.

Also, you can call yourself out of unpleasant situation, like calling yourself out of the grave, out of evil covenants, out of prison of darkness, out of evil marriages, evil association, slavery, and oppression.

2 Corinthians 6:17

17 Wherefore come out from among them, and be ye separate, saith the Lord, and touch not the unclean thing; and I will receive you.

God advise us to come out of Babylon.

Revelation 18:4

4 And I heard another voice from heaven, saying, Come out of her, my people, that ye be not partakers of her sins, and that ye receive not of her plagues.

To come forth is to come out suddenly or forcefully, to escape through a hole or crack like a newborn baby.

Whatever you are passing through God will call you forth if you are willing and obedience.

Your trials and tribulation are not behind him take all to him he will bring you out and you will come forth as gold.

Job 23:10

10 But he knoweth the way that I take: when he hath tried me, I shall come forth as gold.

He will give you strength to bring forth that visions and dream.

Isaiah 37:3

3 And they said unto him, Thus saith Hezekiah, This day is a day of trouble, and of rebuke, and of blasphemy: for the children are come to the birth, and there is not strength to bring forth.

Prayers:

I join my voice to that of the Lord, I call me forth the glory of God to manifest in my life in the name of Yeshua.

My original what are you doing in the graveyard come forth in the name of Yeshua.

My destiny, hear the word of the Lord come out of the grave, come out of evil covenants, evil marriage, evil dedication, prison and cages, evil associations, secret cults, slavery, evil names, come out of Babylon in the name of Yeshua.

My soul come forth from the coven of witchcrafts in the name of Yeshua.

My destiny come out of the dunghills and go and seat among princes in the name of Yeshua.

My wife, my children, my career, my blessings come forth in the name of Yeshua.

CHAPTER 9

LOOSE HIM AND LET HIM GO
John 11:39-44

39 Jesus said, Take ye away the stone. Martha, the sister of him that was dead, saith unto him, Lord, by this time he stinketh: for he hath been dead four days.

40 Jesus saith unto her, Said I not unto thee, that, if thou wouldest believe, thou shouldest see the glory of God?

41 Then they took away the stone from the place where the dead was laid. And Jesus lifted up his eyes, and said, Father, I thank thee that thou hast heard me.

42 And I knew that thou hearest me always: but because of the people which stand by I said it, that they may believe that thou hast sent me.

43 And when he thus had spoken, he cried with a loud voice, Lazarus, come forth.

44 And he that was dead came forth, bound hand and foot with graveclothes: and his face was bound about with a napkin. Jesus saith unto them, Loose him, and let him go.

LOOSE HIM AND LET HIM GO
John 11:44

44 And he that was dead came forth, bound hand and foot with graveclothes: and his face was bound about with a napkin. Jesus saith unto them, Loose him, and let him go.

Surely, Lazarus came forth, but he was still bound with a graveclothes and Yeshua said unto them loose him and let him go.

Many of us are out of the grave but we are still bound or caged in a prison and without being loosed we are as good as dead.

Some are bound by the enemies, some are bound by ancestral covenants and laws, some are bound by religion, some are bound by marriage, and some by curses and spells.

With the power of God, we will be loose.

Yeshua gave the commandment Loose him and let him go, he commanded those who buried him, those who bound him, all the undertakers to loose him and let him go.

The commandment to loose him and let him go in the spirit realm is address to our enemies, it is address to those who bind us, it is address to those stubborn enemies that does not want to let us go.

Pharaoh is a very good example of those stubborn enemies, God told him "Let my people go that they may serve me" but Pharaoh said refuses.

Exodus 5:1-2

1 And afterward Moses and Aaron went in, and told Pharaoh, Thus saith the Lord God of Israel, Let my people go, that they may hold a feast unto me in the wilderness.

2 And Pharaoh said, Who is the Lord, that I should obey his voice to let Israel go? I know not the Lord, neither will I let Israel go.

And we all know the end of the story. The Egyptian were plagued with 10 plagues, until they let Israelite go.

Even the Egyptian pursue them as they let them go, they never let go completely until Pharaoh and his hosts were destroyed in the red sea.

Psalm 136:13-15

13 To him which divided the Red sea into parts: for his mercy endureth for ever:

14 And made Israel to pass through the midst of it: for his mercy endureth for ever:

15 But overthrew Pharaoh and his host in the Red sea: for his mercy endureth for ever.

Some enemy will never let go until God consume them.

Whenever God give the commandment to loose no one can bound or disobey the order or they will loose their lives and the victim will still be deliver.

When God decided it is time to let Israel go from Babylon, the Babylonian refuses to let go, meanwhile it was God who allows them to be taken into captivity in the first place and now the enemies want to continue its hold on them.

They will be claiming the legal right that the Lord has already removed.

Jeremiah 50:7

7 All that found them have devoured them: and their adversaries said, We offend not, because they have sinned against the Lord, the habitation of justice, even the Lord, the hope of their fathers.

They never want to let go without God intervention.

Jeremiah 50:33-34

33 Thus saith the Lord of hosts; The children of Israel and the children of Judah were oppressed together: and all that took them captives held them fast; they refused to let them go.

34 Their Redeemer is strong; the Lord of hosts is his name: he shall throughly plead their cause, that he may give rest to the land, and disquiet the inhabitants of Babylon.

But whenever he decided to deliver no one can stop him.

Isaiah 14:27

27 For the Lord of hosts hath purposed, and who shall disannul it? and his hand is stretched out, and who shall turn it back?

God will fight, destroy, and devour to get your deliverance.

Isaiah 42:14

14 I have long time holden my peace; I have been still, and refrained myself: now will I cry like a travailing woman; I will destroy and devour at once.

God will do anything to deliver you.

Jeremiah 30:16-18

16 Therefore all they that devour thee shall be devoured; and all thine adversaries, every one of them, shall go into captivity; and they that spoil thee shall be a spoil, and all that prey upon thee will I give for a prey.

17 For I will restore health unto thee, and I will heal thee of thy wounds, saith the Lord; because they called thee an Outcast, saying, This is Zion, whom no man seeketh after.

18 Thus saith the Lord; Behold, I will bring again the captivity of Jacob's tents, and have mercy on his dwellingplaces; and the city shall be builded upon her own heap, and the palace shall remain after the manner thereof

God raised an inferior empire Mede-Persian to free Israel from the Babylonians.

Jeremiah 51:1-25

1 Thus saith the Lord; Behold, I will raise up against Babylon, and against them that dwell in the midst of them that rise up against me, a destroying wind;

2 And will send unto Babylon fanners, that shall fan her, and shall empty her land: for in the day of trouble they shall be against her round about.

3 Against him that bendeth let the archer bend his bow, and against him that lifteth himself up in his brigandine: and spare ye not her young men; destroy ye utterly all her host.

4 Thus the slain shall fall in the land of the Chaldeans, and they that are thrust through in her streets.

5 For Israel hath not been forsaken, nor Judah of his God, of the Lord of hosts; though their land was filled with sin against the Holy One of Israel.

6 Flee out of the midst of Babylon, and deliver every man his soul: be not cut off in her iniquity; for this is the time of the Lord's vengeance; he will render unto her a recompence.

7 Babylon hath been a golden cup in the Lord's hand, that made all the earth drunken: the nations have drunken of her wine; therefore the nations are mad.

8 Babylon is suddenly fallen and destroyed: howl for her; take balm for her pain, if so be she may be healed.

9 We would have healed Babylon, but she is not healed: forsake her, and let us go every one into his own country: for her judgment reacheth unto heaven, and is lifted up even to the skies.

10 The Lord hath brought forth our righteousness: come, and let us declare in Zion the work of the Lord our God.

11 Make bright the arrows; gather the shields: the Lord hath raised up the spirit of the kings of the Medes: for his device is against Babylon, to destroy it; because it is the vengeance of the Lord, the vengeance of his temple.

12 Set up the standard upon the walls of Babylon, make the watch strong, set up the watchmen, prepare the ambushes: for the Lord hath both devised and done that which he spake against the inhabitants of Babylon.

13 O thou that dwellest upon many waters, abundant in treasures, thine end is come, and the measure of thy covetousness.

14 The Lord of hosts hath sworn by himself, saying, Surely I will fill thee with men, as with caterpillers; and they shall lift up a shout against thee.

15 He hath made the earth by his power, he hath established the world by his wisdom, and hath stretched out the heaven by his understanding.

16 When he uttereth his voice, there is a multitude of waters in the heavens; and he causeth the vapours to ascend from the ends of the earth: he maketh lightnings with rain, and bringeth forth the wind out of his treasures.

17 Every man is brutish by his knowledge; every founder is confounded by the graven image: for his molten image is falsehood, and there is no breath in them.

18 They are vanity, the work of errors: in the time of their visitation they shall perish.

19 The portion of Jacob is not like them; for he is the former of all things: and Israel is the rod of his inheritance: the Lord of hosts is his name.

20 Thou art my battle axe and weapons of war: for with thee will I break in pieces the nations, and with thee will I destroy kingdoms;

21 And with thee will I break in pieces the horse and his rider; and with thee will I break in pieces the chariot and his rider;

22 With thee also will I break in pieces man and woman; and with thee will I break in pieces old and young; and with thee will I break in pieces the young man and the maid;

23 I will also break in pieces with thee the shepherd and his flock; and with thee will I break in pieces the husbandman and his yoke of oxen; and with thee will I break in pieces captains and rulers.

24 And I will render unto Babylon and to all the inhabitants of Chaldea all their evil that they have done in Zion in your sight, saith the Lord.

25 Behold, I am against thee, O destroying mountain, saith the Lord, which destroyest all the earth: and I will stretch out mine hand upon thee, and roll thee down from the rocks, and will make thee a burnt mountain.

Sometimes, the enemy will loose you but will not let you go, or will not let you go far. The deliverance is not complete when you are not let go completely.

You need to be free and not just free but free indeed.

John 8:36

36 If the Son therefore shall make you free, ye shall be free indeed.

The commandment is loose him and let him go.

DO NOT NEGOTIATE WITH YOUR FREEDOM

Pharaoh was negotiating with the Israelites, he said you are free to go and worship your God but do not go far.

Exodus 8:28

28 And Pharaoh said, I will let you go, that ye may sacrifice to the Lord your God in the wilderness; only ye shall not go very far away: intreat for me.

Again, he said you can go but men alone, no women, no children.

Exodus 10:8-11

8 And Moses and Aaron were brought again unto Pharaoh: and he said unto them, Go, serve the Lordyour God: but who are they that shall go?

9 And Moses said, We will go with our young and with our old, with our sons and with our daughters, with our flocks and with our herds will we go; for we must hold a feast unto the Lord.

10 And he said unto them, Let the Lord be so with you, as I will let you go, and your little ones: look to it; for evil is before you.

11 Not so: go now ye that are men, and serve the Lord; for that ye did desire. And they were driven out from Pharaoh's presence.

Finally, he said, you can go but do not go with your livestock.

Exodus 10:24

24 And Pharaoh called unto Moses, and said, Go ye, serve the Lord; only let your flocks and your herds be stayed: let your little ones also go with you.

In all these Moses never agreed, do not negotiate with your freedom.

Exodus 10:25-29

25 And Moses said, Thou must give us also sacrifices and burnt offerings, that we may sacrifice unto the Lordour God.

26 Our cattle also shall go with us; there shall not an hoof be left behind; for thereof must we take to serve the Lord our God; and we know not with what we must serve the Lord, until we come thither.

27 But the Lord hardened Pharaoh's heart, and he would not let them go.

28 And Pharaoh said unto him, Get thee from me, take heed to thyself, see my face no more; for in that day thou seest my face thou shalt die.

29 And Moses said, Thou hast spoken well, I will see thy face again no more.

And truly they never see his face no more.

Jacob negotiated with Laban, and he worked for 20 years, and Laban still never want to let go until Jacob ran away.

He tricked him to serve 14 years for his two daughters.

Genesis 29:25-30

25 And it came to pass, that in the morning, behold, it was Leah: and he said to Laban, What is this thou hast done unto me? did not I serve with thee for Rachel? wherefore then hast thou beguiled me?

26 And Laban said, It must not be so done in our country, to give the younger before the firstborn.

27 Fulfil her week, and we will give thee this also for the service which thou shalt serve with me yet seven other years.

28 And Jacob did so, and fulfilled her week: and he gave him Rachel his daughter to wife also.

29 And Laban gave to Rachel his daughter Bilhah his handmaid to be her maid.

30 And he went in also unto Rachel, and he loved also Rachel more than Leah, and served with him yet seven other years.

He changes his wages deceitfully 10 times.

Genesis 31:7

7 And your father hath deceived me, and changed my wages ten times; but God suffered him not to hurt me.

The last negotiation favored Jacob because God gave him the idea in the dream.

Genesis 30:25-31

25 And it came to pass, when Rachel had born Joseph, that Jacob said unto Laban, Send me away, that I may go unto mine own place, and to my country.

26 Give me my wives and my children, for whom I have served thee, and let me go: for thou knowest my service which I have done thee.

27 And Laban said unto him, I pray thee, if I have found favour in thine eyes, tarry: for I have learned by experience that the Lordhath blessed me for thy sake.

28 And he said, Appoint me thy wages, and I will give it.

29 And he said unto him, Thou knowest how I have served thee, and how thy cattle was with me.

30 For it was little which thou hadst before I came, and it is now increased unto a multitude; and the Lord hath blessed thee since my coming: and now when shall I provide for mine own house also?

31 And he said, What shall I give thee? And Jacob said, Thou shalt not give me any thing: if thou wilt do this thing for me, I will again feed and keep thy flock.

After the last negotiation Laban countenance change and Jacob had to run at the commandment of God.

Genesis 31:1-3

1 And he heard the words of Laban's sons, saying, Jacob hath taken away all that was our father's; and of that which was our father's hath he gotten all this glory.

2 And Jacob beheld the countenance of Laban, and, behold, it was not toward him as before.

3 And the Lord said unto Jacob, Return unto the land of thy fathers, and to thy kindred; and I will be with thee.

Laban pursued but God did save Jacob by divine intervention and warn Laban in the dream, do not do anything to Jacob.

Genesis 31:24

24 And God came to Laban the Syrian in a dream by night, and said unto him, Take heed that thou speak not to Jacob either good or bad.

Do not negotiate with your freedom, Satan will never want any of his victim to go, but you just must go no matter what, either you are legally or illegally captured, your God will contend with them.

Isaiah 49:24-26

24 Shall the prey be taken from the mighty, or the lawful captive delivered?

25 But thus saith the Lord, Even the captives of the mighty shall be taken away, and the prey of the terrible shall be delivered: for I will contend with him that contendeth with thee, and I will save thy children.

26 And I will feed them that oppress thee with their own flesh; and they shall be drunken with their own blood, as with sweet wine: and all flesh shall know that I the Lord am thy Saviour and thy Redeemer, the mighty One of Jacob.

Prayers:

Pharaoh of my father's house / mother's house loose me and let me go in the name of Yeshua.

Witchcraft powers assign against my life and destiny loose me and let me go in the name of Yeshua.

Marine powers power assign against my life and destiny loose me and let me go in the name of Yeshua.

Ancestral and generational evil covenant upon my life and destiny loose me and let me go in the name of Yeshua.

Power of evil dedication against my life and destiny loose me and let me go in the name of Yeshua.

Spirit of failure, loneliness, shame, oppression, afflictions, death, debt, poverty, vagabond, Beelzebub, witchcrafts and disgrace hear the word of the Lord loose me and let me go in the name of Yeshua.

Graveyards hear the word of the Lord loose me and let me go in the name of Yeshua.

Babylonian spirit, hear the word of the Lord loose me and let me go in the name of Yeshua.

Father, pay divine visitation to those that does not want to let me go in the name of Yeshua.

Anyone that can harm me, every enemy that are stronger than me, Father, warn them as you warn Laban to leave me alone in the name of Yeshua.

CHAPTER 10

HELP

In this life we all need help in this life, without help we are as good as dead.

John 11:39-44

39 Jesus said, Take ye away the stone. Martha, the sister of him that was dead, saith unto him, Lord, by this time he stinketh: for he hath been dead four days.

40 Jesus saith unto her, Said I not unto thee, that, if thou wouldest believe, thou shouldest see the glory of God?

41 Then they took away the stone from the place where the dead was laid. And Jesus lifted up his eyes, and said, Father, I thank thee that thou hast heard me.

42 And I knew that thou hearest me always: but because of the people which stand by I said it, that they may believe that thou hast sent me.

43 And when he thus had spoken, he cried with a loud voice, Lazarus, come forth.

44 And he that was dead came forth, bound hand and foot with graveclothes: and his face was bound about with a napkin. Jesus saith unto them, Loose him, and let him go.

When you look at all the circumstances that surrounded Lazarus death and resurrection you will see that there is absolutely nothing, he can do about them.

While he was sick his sisters have done the necessary thing by sending message to Yeshua that your friend Lazarus is sick.

John 11:3

3 Therefore his sisters sent unto him, saying, Lord, behold, he whom thou lovest is sick.

He also needs help for the stone to be taken away.

He needs help to be risen by Yeshua's prayer.

He needs help to be loosed.

The only place where he can help himself is to go after being loosed.

We all need help in life, without help we cannot do anything meaningful in life.

SOURCES OF HELP

The only source of help is God, but they are in three dimensions.

1 GOD

Whenever we need help our first place to go is to God himself. Go to God in prayers.

Lazarus's sisters went to God in prayers, they sent to Yeshua for help.

John 11:3

3 Therefore his sisters sent unto him, saying, Lord, behold, he whom thou lovest is sick.

David said in Psalm 121 that I will lift up my eyes unto the Lord, from where cometh my help and in the end he said it is the Lord that will preserve him forever.

Psalm 121

1 I will lift up mine eyes unto the hills, from whence cometh my help.

2 My help cometh from the Lord, which made heaven and earth.

3 He will not suffer thy foot to be moved: he that keepeth thee will not slumber.

4 Behold, he that keepeth Israel shall neither slumber nor sleep.

5 The Lord is thy keeper: the Lord is thy shade upon thy right hand.

6 The sun shall not smite thee by day, nor the moon by night.

7 The Lord shall preserve thee from all evil: he shall preserve thy soul.

8 The Lord shall preserve thy going out and thy coming in from this time forth, and even for evermore.

In Psalm 124 David let us know that it is the Lord that help us from our enemies, because they are stronger than we are. But through the help of God, they cannot swallow us, they cannot overwhelm us, their snare is broken with help of God so we can escape.

Psalm 124

1 If it had not been the Lord who was on our side, now may Israel say;

2 If it had not been the Lordwho was on our side, when men rose up against us:

3 Then they had swallowed us up quick, when their wrath was kindled against us:

4 Then the waters had overwhelmed us, the stream had gone over our soul:

5 Then the proud waters had gone over our soul.

6 Blessed be the Lord, who hath not given us as a prey to their teeth.

7 Our soul is escaped as a bird out of the snare of the fowlers: the snare is broken, and we are escaped.

8 Our help is in the name of the Lord, who made heaven and earth.

2 GOD, THROUGH ANGELS

Our second source of help is God, through his angels.

Angels are needed to roll away spiritual stone place on us, they are needed to break snares and cages. It was the angel that roll away the stone from Yeshua's tomb.

Matthew 28:2

2 And, behold, there was a great earthquake: for the angel of the Lord descended from heaven, and came and rolled back the stone from the door, and sat upon it.

We all have ministering angels and in addition God send special angels to us to do some special assignment on our behalf.

Hebrews 1:14

14 Are they not all ministering spirits, sent forth to minister for them who shall be heirs of salvation?

God sometimes send angel as men for a certain purpose in our life and they left after that assignment is over. We have to be prayerful always, so we don't neglect our angels.

Hebrews 13:2

2 Be not forgetful to entertain strangers: for thereby some have entertained angels unawares.

Angels are very important; all the battles are fought by the angels of God.

Revelation 12:7-9

7 And there was war in heaven: Michael and his angels fought against the dragon; and the dragon fought and his angels,

8 And prevailed not; neither was their place found any more in heaven.

9 And the great dragon was cast out, that old serpent, called the Devil, and Satan, which deceiveth the whole world: he was cast out into the earth, and his angels were cast out with him.

Just one angel destroyed 185,000 armies of Sennacherib.

Isaiah 37:36

36 Then the angel of the Lord went forth, and smote in the camp of the Assyrians a hundred and fourscore and five thousand: and when they arose early in the morning, behold, they were all dead corpses.

All our prayers and answers to our prayers are being carried up and down simultaneously by the angels.

Genesis 28:12

12 And he dreamed, and behold a ladder set up on the earth, and the top of it reached to heaven: and behold the angels of God ascending and descending on it.

The only time God come down is when you give him quality praise in trouble just like Paul and Silas in the prison.

Acts 16:25-26

25 And at midnight Paul and Silas prayed, and sang praises unto God: and the prisoners heard them.

26 And suddenly there was a great earthquake, so that the foundations of the prison were shaken: and immediately all the doors were opened, and every one's bands were loosed.

3 GOD, THROUGH MEN

The third source of help is God through men.

God will use men to bless us physically on this earth.

Men cannot truly help us without the help of God, if they do, they will want something in return for vain is the help of man.

Psalm 108:12-13

12 Give us help from trouble: for vain is the help of man.

13 Through God we shall do valiantly: for he it is that shall tread down our enemies.

Except it is from God it is vain.

Psalm 127:1

1 Except the Lord build the house, they labour in vain that build it: except the Lord keep the city, the watchman waketh but in vain.

You must not trust men but trust God for men.

Believe it or not everything we get in life are from God.

John 3:27

27 John answered and said, A man can receive nothing, except it be given him from heaven.

James 1:17

17 Every good gift and every perfect gift is from above, and cometh down from the Father of lights, with whom is no variableness, neither shadow of turning.

God will send men to help us as we begin to do his will but it is a curse to put your trust in men for you will never see things for yourself but forever rely on men and men will be disappointing you.

Jeremiah 17:5-6

5 Thus saith the Lord; Cursed be the man that trusteth in man, and maketh flesh his arm, and whose heart departeth from the Lord.

6 For he shall be like the heath in the desert, and shall not see when good cometh; but shall inhabit the parched places in the wilderness, in a salt land and not inhabited.

But when your hope is on the Lord to send help then you are blessed.

Jeremiah 17:7-8

7 Blessed is the man that trusteth in the Lord, and whose hope the Lord is.

8 For he shall be as a tree planted by the waters, and that spreadeth out her roots by the river, and shall not see when heat cometh, but her leaf shall be green; and shall not be careful in the year of drought, neither shall cease from yielding fruit.

So, in all things lift up your head to the hills for there your help comes from.

Prayers:

Father, I am helpless send help in the name of Yeshua.

Father, you are the helper of the helpless, help me in the name of Yeshua.

My destiny helper, where are you? Locate me in the name of Yeshua.

Father, you have been a strength to the poor, a strength to the needy help me to overpower this storm in the name of Yeshua.

Father your word says your grace is sufficient for me, overshadow me with grace all the days of my life in the name of Yeshua.

CHAPTER 11

WOMAN THOU ART LOOSE

Luke 13:10-17

10 And he was teaching in one of the synagogues on the sabbath.

11 And, behold, there was a woman which had a spirit of infirmity eighteen years, and was bowed together, and could in no wise lift up herself.

12 And when Jesus saw her, he called her to him, and said unto her, Woman, thou art loosed from thine infirmity.

13 And he laid his hands on her: and immediately she was made straight, and glorified God.

14 And the ruler of the synagogue answered with indignation, because that Jesus had healed on the sabbath day, and said unto the people, There are six days in which men ought to work: in them therefore come and be healed, and not on the sabbath day.

15 The Lord then answered him, and said, Thou hypocrite, doth not each one of you on the sabbath loose his ox or his ass from the stall, and lead him away to watering?

16 And ought not this woman, being a daughter of Abraham, whom Satan hath bound, lo, these eighteen years, be loosed from this bond on the sabbath day?

17 And when he had said these things, all his adversaries were ashamed: and all the people rejoiced for all the glorious things that were done by him.

In John chapter 11 the Lord delivered a man named Lazarus here in Luke chapter 13 it was the turn of a woman.

It was on a sabbath day when men are not supposed to work but rest and meditate on the word of the Lord.

Exodus 20:8-11

8 Remember the sabbath day, to keep it holy.

9 Six days shalt thou labour, and do all thy work:

10 But the seventh day is the sabbath of the Lord thy God: in it thou shalt not do any work, thou, nor thy son, nor thy daughter, thy manservant, nor thy maidservant, nor thy cattle, nor thy stranger that is within thy gates:

11 For in six days the Lord made heaven and earth, the sea, and all that in them is, and rested the seventh day: wherefore the Lord blessed the sabbath day, and hallowed it.

But as he was teaching, Yeshua saw what he came to do (to set the captive free). He saw a woman with spirit of infirmity, and he immediately delivered her.

Luke 13:11-13

11 And, behold, there was a woman which had a spirit of infirmity eighteen years, and was bowed together, and could in no wise lift up herself.

12 And when Jesus saw her, he called her to him, and said unto her, Woman, thou art loosed from thine infirmity.

13 And he laid his hands on her: and immediately she was made straight, and glorified God.

Yeshua knew the ruler will not be happy, but he cannot leave his sheep unattended to. The rulers of the synagogue truly were not happy, they were not taking it lightly with him because he has healed on the sabbath day. They were mad because one of their preys is gone.

Luke 13:14

14 And the ruler of the synagogue answered with indignation, because that Jesus had healed on the sabbath day, and said unto the people, There are six days in which men ought to work: in them therefore come and be healed, and not on the sabbath day.

They were saying, if anyone is dying on the sabbath day let him die because it is on the sabbath day.

And Yeshua answered them properly, we are not supposed to work on sabbath day, but you lead your cattle to the water on a sabbath day that is equally working. Now I am doing the same thing to my sheep that needed attention and you are complaining.

Luke 13:15-16

15 The Lord then answered him, and said, Thou hypocrite, doth not each one of you on the sabbath loose his ox or his ass from the stall, and lead him away to watering?

16 And ought not this woman, being a daughter of Abraham, whom Satan hath bound, lo, these eighteen years, be loosed from this bond on the sabbath day?

He was trying to explain to them man or animal which is more important?

This issue of healing on the sabbath day had occurred between him and the Pharisees at one point and his argument was the same, you rescued and feed your cattle on the sabbath day how much more is human (my sheep) which are more important than the animals.

Matthew 12:10-14

10 And, behold, there was a man which had his hand withered. And they asked him, saying, Is it lawful to heal on the sabbath days? that they might accuse him.

11 And he said unto them, What man shall there be among you, that shall have one sheep, and if it fall into a pit on the sabbath day, will he not lay hold on it, and lift it out?

12 How much then is a man better than a sheep? Wherefore it is lawful to do well on the sabbath days.

13 Then saith he to the man, Stretch forth thine hand. And he stretched it forth; and it was restored whole, like as the other.

14 Then the Pharisees went out, and held a council against him, how they might destroy him.

Just as it was before Yeshua came, to this world, the rulers' feeds on the needs of the poor, they will rather keep you poor so you can depend on them.

Amos 5:6-12

6 Seek the Lord, and ye shall live; lest he break out like fire in the house of Joseph, and devour it, and there be none to quench it in Bethel.

7 Ye who turn judgment to wormwood, and leave off righteousness in the earth,

8 Seek him that maketh the seven stars and Orion, and turneth the shadow of death into the morning, and maketh the day dark with night: that calleth for the waters of the sea, and poureth them out upon the face of the earth: The Lord is his name:

9 That strengtheneth the spoiled against the strong, so that the spoiled shall come against the fortress.

10 They hate him that rebuketh in the gate, and they abhor him that speaketh uprightly.

11 Forasmuch therefore as your treading is upon the poor, and ye take from him burdens of wheat: ye have built houses of hewn stone, but ye shall not dwell in them; ye have planted pleasant vineyards, but ye shall not drink wine of them.

12 For I know your manifold transgressions and your mighty sins: they afflict the just, they take a bribe, and they turn aside the poor in the gate from their right.

So, it was in his time, they never change because they are of the devil, and he said it to their face.

John 8:44

44 Ye are of your father the devil, and the lusts of your father ye will do. He was a murderer from the beginning, and abode not in the truth, because there is no truth in him. When he speaketh a lie, he speaketh of his own: for he is a liar, and the father of it.

And so, it is now, people never change, and they are getting even worst as we are approaching the end time.

Satan their father is the same yesterday, today and till the second coming of the Lord.

2 Timothy 3:1-7

1 This know also, that in the last days perilous times shall come.

2 For men shall be lovers of their own selves, covetous, boasters, proud, blasphemers, disobedient to parents, unthankful, unholy,

3 Without natural affection, trucebreakers, false accusers, incontinent, fierce, despisers of those that are good,

4 Traitors, heady, highminded, lovers of pleasures more than lovers of God;

5 Having a form of godliness, but denying the power thereof: from such turn away.

6 For of this sort are they which creep into houses, and lead captive silly women laden with sins, led away with divers lusts,

7 Ever learning, and never able to come to the knowledge of the truth.

The wicked will never let go, it is God that set us free by his power. They will prefer for their animals to leave for you to die. They lay unnecessary burdens on men.

Matthew 23:4

4 For they bind heavy burdens and grievous to be borne, and lay them on men's shoulders; but they themselves will not move them with one of their fingers.

Only Yeshua can remove these burdens.

Matthew 11:28-30

28 Come unto me, all ye that labour and are heavy laden, and I will give you rest.

29 Take my yoke upon you, and learn of me; for I am meek and lowly in heart: and ye shall find rest unto your souls.

30 For my yoke is easy, and my burden is light.

Yeshua pointed out the special reason to them "ought not this woman, being a daughter of Abraham", daughter of Abraham then is referring to the true child of God.

Luke 13:16

16 And ought not this woman, being a daughter of Abraham, whom Satan hath bound, lo, these eighteen years, be loosed from this bond on the sabbath day?

The ruler realized that they had nothing to prove they left shamefully, and the regular people rejoice for someone is able to speak the truth.

Luke 13:17

17 And when he had said these things, all his adversaries were ashamed: and all the people rejoiced for all the glorious things that were done by him.

YESHUA IS THE GOOD SHEPERD

Yeshua is the good shepherd, he will take care of his sheep, he will take care of us.

John 10:11-18

11 I am the good shepherd: the good shepherd giveth his life for the sheep.

12 But he that is an hireling, and not the shepherd, whose own the sheep are not, seeth the wolf coming, and leaveth the sheep, and fleeth: and the wolf catcheth them, and scattereth the sheep.

13 The hireling fleeth, because he is an hireling, and careth not for the sheep.

14 I am the good shepherd, and know my sheep, and am known of mine.

15 As the Father knoweth me, even so know I the Father: and I lay down my life for the sheep.

16 And other sheep I have, which are not of this fold: them also I must bring, and they shall hear my voice; and there shall be one fold, and one shepherd.

17 Therefore doth my Father love me, because I lay down my life, that I might take it again.

18 No man taketh it from me, but I lay it down of myself. I have power to lay it down, and I have power to take it again. This commandment have I received of my Father.

HE CAME TO DELIVER US FROM SATANIC BONDAGES

Luke 4:18-19

18 The Spirit of the Lord is upon me, because he hath anointed me to preach the gospel to the poor; he hath sent me to heal the brokenhearted, to preach deliverance to the captives, and recovering of sight to the blind, to set at liberty them that are bruised,

19 To preach the acceptable year of the Lord.

HE IS THE LORD OF THE SABBATH

Yeshua is the Lord of the sabbath, and this gives him right to work on the sabbath day, but he never breaks the laws but rather he came to fulfil the law, so that we can be free.

Matthew 12:1-8

1 At that time Jesus went on the sabbath day through the corn; and his disciples were an hungred, and began to pluck the ears of corn and to eat.

2 But when the Pharisees saw it, they said unto him, Behold, thy disciples do that which is not lawful to do upon the sabbath day.

3 But he said unto them, Have ye not read what David did, when he was an hungred, and they that were with him;

4 How he entered into the house of God, and did eat the shewbread, which was not lawful for him to eat, neither for them which were with him, but only for the priests?

5 Or have ye not read in the law, how that on the sabbath days the priests in the temple profane the sabbath, and are blameless?

6 But I say unto you, That in this place is one greater than the temple.

7 But if ye had known what this meaneth, I will have mercy, and not sacrifice, ye would not have condemned the guiltless.

8 For the Son of man is Lord even of the sabbath day.

He told them categorically; I am the end of the law of Moses.

Romans 10:4

4 For Christ is the end of the law for righteousness to every one that believeth.

I came to fulfil it for you once and for all.

Matthew 5:17

17 Think not that I am come to destroy the law, or the prophets: I am not come to destroy, but to fulfil.

You cannot fulfil the law, but I came to fulfil it that you can become righteous.

Romans 8:3-4

3 For what the law could not do, in that it was weak through the flesh, God sending his own Son in the likeness of sinful flesh, and for sin, condemned sin in the flesh:

4 That the righteousness of the law might be fulfilled in us, who walk not after the flesh, but after the Spirit.

No one can fulfil the ten laws on his own and if you break one you break all.

James 2:10

10 For whosoever shall keep the whole law, and yet offend in one point, he is guilty of all.

Prayers:

Joshua Oluyomi Olumoye (put your name) thou art loose from thine infirmities in the name of Yeshua.

Every tongue that shall rise up against me are condemn in the name of Yeshua.

Judgement of darkness upon my life be terminated by the mercy of God in the name of Yeshua.

CHAPTER 12

WHY MUST THEY LET YOU GO? (PURPOSE OF FREEDOM)

Though we have gone astray but God chooses to set us free. There are several reasons why God decided to set us free.

1 LOVE

The love that God has for mankind from the beginning is what prompted him to set us free.

John 3:16

16 For God so loved the world, that he gave his only begotten Son, that whosoever believeth in him should not perish, but have everlasting life.

Men have gone astray; we are all doing what we like but, in our sins, he chooses to die for us because of love.

Romans 5:8

8 But God commendeth his love toward us, in that, while we were yet sinners, Christ died for us.

Out of this love come grace that spare Noah and his family from the flood for God wanted to destroy us all.

Genesis 6:5-8

5 And God saw that the wickedness of man was great in the earth, and that every imagination of the thoughts of his heart was only evil continually.

6 And it repented the Lord that he had made man on the earth, and it grieved him at his heart.

7 And the Lord said, I will destroy man whom I have created from the face of the earth; both man, and beast, and the creeping thing, and the fowls of the air; for it repenteth me that I have made them.

8 But Noah found grace in the eyes of the Lord.

And the product of this love and grace is mercy through which God was able to relate again to a sinful man or we will be consumed because we are stiff necked.

Exodus 25:21-22

21 And thou shalt put the mercy seat above upon the ark; and in the ark thou shalt put the testimony that I shall give thee.

22 And there I will meet with thee, and I will commune with thee from above the mercy seat, from between the two cherubims which are upon the ark of the testimony, of all things which I will give thee in commandment unto the children of Israel.

Hence the mercy seat and the mercy seat became Yeshua and Yeshua's death open the mercy seat for us as the throne of grace so we can obtain mercy.

Hebrews 4:14-16

14 Seeing then that we have a great high priest, that is passed into the heavens, Jesus the Son of God, let us hold fast our profession.

15 For we have not an high priest which cannot be touched with the feeling of our infirmities; but was in all points tempted like as we are, yet without sin.

16 Let us therefore come boldly unto the throne of grace, that we may obtain mercy, and find grace to help in time of need.

Our response is to love him back because he first loved us.

1 John 4:19

19 We love him, because he first loved us.

2 TO SERVE GOD

Our primary purpose of creation initially was to serve the Lord just like the angels in the heaven and our secondary assignment is in the blessings and commandment given to Adam and Eve in Genesis 1.

Genesis 1:28

28 And God blessed them, and God said unto them, Be fruitful, and multiply, and replenish the earth, and subdue it: and have dominion over the fish of the sea, and over the fowl of the air, and over every living thing that moveth upon the earth.

Unfortunately, Satan cunningly took all from Adam and hence we are all in bondage to Satan through sin.

Romans 5:12

12 Wherefore, as by one man sin entered into the world, and death by sin; and so death passed upon all men, for that all have sinned:

Now God is back to save us, but we must know that the purpose of salvation is still the same, and that purpose is to serve him.

When he decided to save Israel, he told Pharaoh "let my people go that they may serve."

Exodus 5:1-2

1 And afterward Moses and Aaron went in, and told Pharaoh, Thus saith the Lord God of Israel, Let my people go, that they may hold a feast unto me in the wilderness.

2 And Pharaoh said, Who is the Lord, that I should obey his voice to let Israel go? I know not the Lord, neither will I let Israel go.

There are several ways to serve the Lord, but basically to serve the Lord

We must reciprocate his love by loving him with all our earth and recognize his Lordship over our lives and to him alone must be our worship.

Deuteronomy 6:4-5

4 Hear, O Israel: The Lord our God is one Lord:

5 And thou shalt love the Lord thy God with all thine heart, and with all thy soul, and with all thy might.

If you love him, you cannot share him with another gods

Exodus 20:3-5

3 Thou shalt have no other gods before me.

4 Thou shalt not make unto thee any graven image, or any likeness of any thing that is in heaven above, or that is in the earth beneath, or that is in the water under the earth.

5 Thou shalt not bow down thyself to them, nor serve them: for I the Lord thy God am a jealous God, visiting the iniquity of the fathers upon the children unto the third and fourth generation of them that hate me;

When we share him, we are deceiving ourselves for we already leave him for the other.

Matthew 6:24

24 No man can serve two masters: for either he will hate the one, and love the other; or else he will hold to the one, and despise the other. Ye cannot serve God and mammon.

Secondly, we must do his will by keeping his commandments and be in agreement with him.

Deuteronomy 13:4

4 Ye shall walk after the Lord your God, and fear him, and keep his commandments, and obey his voice, and ye shall serve him, and cleave unto him.

Amos 3:3

3 Can two walk together, except they be agreed?

Thirdly, you serve him in prayers, thanksgiving, praise and worship. Seeking his face always. Worship him in truth and in spirit.

Matthew 6:33

33 But seek ye first the kingdom of God, and his righteousness; and all these things shall be added unto you.

John 4:24

24 God is a Spirit: and they that worship him must worship him in spirit and in truth.

1 Thessalonians 5:16-18

16 Rejoice evermore.

17 Pray without ceasing.

18 In every thing give thanks: for this is the will of God in Christ Jesus concerning you.

Ephesians 5:19-20

19 Speaking to yourselves in psalms and hymns and spiritual songs, singing and making melody in your heart to the Lord;

20 Giving thanks always for all things unto God and the Father in the name of our Lord Jesus Christ;

3 THE LORD HAS NEED OF US
Luke 19:29-35

29 And it came to pass, when he was come nigh to Bethphage and Bethany, at the mount called the mount of Olives, he sent two of his disciples,

30 Saying, Go ye into the village over against you; in the which at your entering ye shall find a colt tied, whereon yet never man sat: loose him, and bring him hither.

31 And if any man ask you, Why do ye loose him? thus shall ye say unto him, Because the Lord hath need of him.

32 And they that were sent went their way, and found even as he had said unto them.

33 And as they were loosing the colt, the owners thereof said unto them, Why loose ye the colt?

34 And they said, The Lord hath need of him.

35 And they brought him to Jesus: and they cast their garments upon the colt, and they set Jesus thereon.

Your freedom has a little cost and that is you carrying Yeshua. The tied colt in the scriptures above can only be free as long as Yeshua is going to ride on it.

As a believer we must know that our freedom is not without a cost., we have Yeshua's to carry, living holy, praying, and fasting regularly, helping others even when is not convenient and many other good things that we are not used to.

The moment you leave the camp of Satan all hell will break loose; Satan will wage war, and this might weigh you down if you do not know beforehand.

Yeshua told his disciples what will happen to them after so they can prepare. The good news about this is that we will overcome because he overcame.

John 16:33

33 These things I have spoken unto you, that in me ye might have peace. In the world ye shall have tribulation: but be of good cheer; I have overcome the world.

This is unavoidable sharing of his suffering that will precedes sharing of his glory.

If he does nor ride on you something else will ride on you

And the good news is he is not too heavy as we think, he said my yoke is easy and my burden I light (Mathew 11:28-30).

1 Peter 4:13

13 But rejoice, inasmuch as ye are partakers of Christ's sufferings; that, when his glory shall be revealed, ye may be glad also with exceeding joy.

Paul calls it light affliction for a moment, though spiritual battles is part of us till the second coming, but you will get to a stage where it will be nothing to you and soon you will be helping others in such situation.

2 Corinthians 4:17

17 For our light affliction, which is but for a moment, worketh for us a far more exceeding and eternal weight of glory;

All these are part of the yokes and burden of Yeshua. Yeshua and Satan, they both have yokes and burdens, but one is lighter the other is heavy.

Matthew 11:28-30

28 Come unto me, all ye that labour and are heavy laden, and I will give you rest.

29 Take my yoke upon you, and learn of me; for I am meek and lowly in heart: and ye shall find rest unto your souls.

30 For my yoke is easy, and my burden is light.

He says come from under that heavy burden and be free from slavery and take this little yoke and begin your rest.

Is from one captivity to another captivity but the latter is better, the latter leads to eternal life.

Ephesians 4:8

8 Wherefore he saith, When he ascended up on high, he led captivity captive, and gave gifts unto men.

Translation from the power of darkness to the kingdom of light.

Colossians 1:13-14

13 Who hath delivered us from the power of darkness, and hath translated us into the kingdom of his dear Son:

14 In whom we have redemption through his blood, even the forgiveness of sins:

4 TO FULFIL YOUR DESTINY

Jeremiah 29:11

11 For I know the thoughts that I think toward you, saith the Lord, thoughts of peace, and not of evil, to give you an expected end.

Our destiny is our expected end in life. Every man has book that is written of him in the heaven.

Hebrews 10:7

7 Then said I, Lo, I come (in the volume of the book it is written of me,) to do thy will, O God.

He brought us out, to bring us in to our destiny.

Deuteronomy 6:23

23 And he brought us out from thence, that he might bring us in, to give us the land which he sware unto our fathers.

God has created us with a purpose, but this purpose was changed by Satan, and we are all heading in a wrong direction.

The foundation of the world has been changed and we are all going to hell.

Psalm 82:5

5 They know not, neither will they understand; they walk on in darkness: all the foundations of the earth are out of course.

But God came to get our freedom so we can fulfill our destiny, which is making heaven in the end.

He knew us for he designed us from birth to death.

Psalm 139:16

16 Thine eyes did see my substance, yet being unperfect; and in thy book all my members were written, which in continuance were fashioned, when as yet there was none of them.

We are foreknown and we are predestined by him.

Romans 8:29-30

29 For whom he did foreknow, he also did predestinate to be conformed to the image of his Son, that he might be the firstborn among many brethren.

30 Moreover whom he did predestinate, them he also called: and whom he called, them he also justified: and whom he justified, them he also glorified.

Satan came so we don't fulfill our destiny, but Yeshua came so we can fulfil our destiny, to live life and have abundant of life, which is eternal life.

John 10:10

10 The thief cometh not, but for to steal, and to kill, and to destroy: I am come that they might have life, and that they might have it more abundantly.

5 TO ESTABLISH THE KINGDOM OF GOD ON EARTH

Apart from serving the Lord men were created to establish the kingdom of God on earth.

God is particular about his kingdom on earth, as Yeshua thought us in the Lord's prayer "thy kingdom come" because the kingdom is not yet come until the second coming, but we have to prepare souls for the kingdom.

Matthew 6:9-13

9 After this manner therefore pray ye: Our Father which art in heaven, Hallowed be thy name.

10 Thy kingdom come, Thy will be done in earth, as it is in heaven.

11 Give us this day our daily bread.

12 And forgive us our debts, as we forgive our debtors.

13 And lead us not into temptation, but deliver us from evil: For thine is the kingdom, and the power, and the glory, for ever. Amen.

We are the physical manifestation of God, when he created us, he created us in his image. Everything other beings in heaven and on heart are spiritual, only Yeshua has human nature, only Yeshua has blood, all the angels have no blood.

They all need men to carry on in the physical, that is why the battle over men is tough. Satan was jealous that men will reign on earth, so he took over.

But the plan never changes we are set free and empowered to preach about the true kingdom for the Son of man is coming back to rule and we will reign with him in his kingdom.

Acts 1:8

8 But ye shall receive power, after that the Holy Ghost is come upon you: and ye shall be witnesses unto me both in Jerusalem, and in all Judaea, and in Samaria, and unto the uttermost part of the earth.

6 TO SHOW SATAN THAT HE (GOD) HAS THE FINAL SAY

Satan because of pride and greed has decided to be like God and get the worship from men, but while he was still pondering the thought in his heart God told him he will fail at the end.

Isaiah 14:12-15

12 How art thou fallen from heaven, O Lucifer, son of the morning! how art thou cut down to the ground, which didst weaken the nations!

13 For thou hast said in thine heart, I will ascend into heaven, I will exalt my throne above the stars of God: I will sit also upon the mount of the congregation, in the sides of the north:

14 I will ascend above the heights of the clouds; I will be like the most High.

15 Yet thou shalt be brought down to hell, to the sides of the pit.

Satan is the ruler of this world, but he does not have the final say over the children of God. For it is God who ultimately rules in the affairs of men and not Satan.

Daniel 4:17

17 This matter is by the decree of the watchers, and the demand by the word of the holy ones: to the intent that the living may know that the most High ruleth in the kingdom of men, and giveth it to whomsoever he will, and setteth up over it the basest of men.

God is the final judge in any matter concerning men and not Satan.

Psalm 75:6-7

6 For promotion cometh neither from the east, nor from the west, nor from the south.

7 But God is the judge: he putteth down one, and setteth up another.

Yeshua emphasized the same truth before the Roman ruler and governor, Pontius Pilate, when he told him he had no power over him but God.

John 19:10-11

10 Then saith Pilate unto him, Speakest thou not unto me? knowest thou not that I have power to crucify thee, and have power to release thee?

11 Jesus answered, Thou couldest have no power at all against me, except it were given thee from above: therefore he that delivered me unto thee hath the greater sin.

Satan is limited to the boundary given to him by God, though he contends with the believers he will not get you if you did not yield to his temptation.

Job 1:12

12 And the Lord said unto Satan, Behold, all that he hath is in thy power; only upon himself put not forth thine hand. So Satan went forth from the presence of the Lord.

God had the final say over stubborn Pharaoh.

Exodus 14:16-18

16 But lift thou up thy rod, and stretch out thine hand over the sea, and divide it: and the children of Israel shall go on dry ground through the midst of the sea.

17 And I, behold, I will harden the hearts of the Egyptians, and they shall follow them: and I will get me honour upon Pharaoh, and upon all his host, upon his chariots, and upon his horsemen.

18 And the Egyptians shall know that I am the Lord, when I have gotten me honour upon Pharaoh, upon his chariots, and upon his horsemen.

God had the final say over arrogant Sennacherib, God told him I will put a hook in your nose and turn you back.

Isaiah 37:29

29 Because thy rage against me, and thy tumult, is come up into mine ears, therefore will I put my hook in thy nose, and my bridle in thy lips, and I will turn thee back by the way by which thou camest.

God will do anything to save his beloved, to save the believers. God defended Judah and just on angel killed 185,000 armies overnight and Sennacherib end his life through homicide.

Isaiah 37:36-38

36 Then the angel of the Lord went forth, and smote in the camp of the Assyrians a hundred and fourscore and five thousand: and when they arose early in the morning, behold, they were all dead corpses.

37 So Sennacherib king of Assyria departed, and went and returned, and dwelt at Nineveh.

38 And it came to pass, as he was worshipping in the house of Nisroch his god, that Adrammelech and Sharezer his sons smote him with the sword; and they escaped into the land of Armenia: and Esarhaddon his son reigned in his stead.

What about Goliath? What about Haman? What about king Herod? God had the final say over them all.

7 FOR HIS GLORY

Finally, the Lord deliver us to get him glory. God does not joke with his glory; men were created for his glory.

Isaiah 43:7

7 Even every one that is called by my name: for I have created him for my glory, I have formed him; yea, I have made him.

And he chooses to deliver us for his glory.

Isaiah 61:1-3

1 The Spirit of the Lord God is upon me; because the Lord hath anointed me to preach good tidings unto the meek; he hath sent me to bind up the brokenhearted, to proclaim liberty to the captives, and the opening of the prison to them that are bound;

2 To proclaim the acceptable year of the Lord, and the day of vengeance of our God; to comfort all that mourn;

3 To appoint unto them that mourn in Zion, to give unto them beauty for ashes, the oil of joy for mourning, the garment of praise for the spirit of heaviness; that they might be called trees of righteousness, the planting of the Lord, that he might be glorified.

The commandment to arise and shine in Isaiah 60 is all for his glory.

Isaiah 60:1-2

1 Arise, shine; for thy light is come, and the glory of the Lord is risen upon thee.

2 For, behold, the darkness shall cover the earth, and gross darkness the people: but the Lord shall arise upon thee, and his glory shall be seen upon thee.

For His glory to be revealed he smoothen our ways.

Isaiah 40:4-5

4 Every valley shall be exalted, and every mountain and hill shall be made low: and the crooked shall be made straight, and the rough places plain:

5 And the glory of the Lord shall be revealed, and all flesh shall see it together: for the mouth of the Lord hath spoken it.

He hardened Pharaoh's heart to get him glory and honor.

Exodus 14:17-18

17 And I, behold, I will harden the hearts of the Egyptians, and they shall follow them: and I will get me honour upon Pharaoh, and upon all his host, upon his chariots, and upon his horsemen.

18 And the Egyptians shall know that I am the Lord, when I have gotten me honour upon Pharaoh, upon his chariots, and upon his horsemen.

He made us light that he might be glorified.

Matthew 5:14-16

14 Ye are the light of the world. A city that is set on an hill cannot be hid.

15 Neither do men light a candle, and put it under a bushel, but on a candlestick; and it giveth light unto all that are in the house.

16 Let your light so shine before men, that they may see your good works, and glorify your Father which is in heaven.

He keeps us alive to declare His glory.

Psalm 118:17

17 I shall not die, but live, and declare the works of the Lord.

He said the sickness of Lazarus is for the glory of God

John 11:4

4 When Jesus heard that, he said, This sickness is not unto death, but for the glory of God, that the Son of God might be glorified thereby.

He is the glory and the lifter of our head.

Psalm 3:3

3 But thou, O Lord, art a shield for me; my glory, and the lifter up of mine head.

All glory, the excellency of power must be return to him who has bestow so much glory on us.

2 Corinthians 4:6-7

6 For God, who commanded the light to shine out of darkness, hath shined in our hearts, to give the light of the knowledge of the glory of God in the face of Jesus Christ.

7 But we have this treasure in earthen vessels, that the excellency of the power may be of God, and not of us.

Prayers:

I love you Lord and I declare and decree that all things begin to work together for my good in the name of Yeshua.

The Lord give life for my life because he loved me.

I enforce the will and the kingdom of God over my life and situations in the name of Yeshua.

Pharaoh of my father's house, Pharaoh of my mother's house, release me for the Lord has need of me in the name of Yeshua.

Whoever has stagnated and bound me in one spot release my life because the Lord has need of me.

Satan you lose, because it is the Lord that has the final say over my life and destiny in the name of Yeshua.

I will not die but live to declare the glory of the Lord in the name of Yeshua.

CHAPTER 13

MAINTAINING YOUR FREEDOM

Maintaining your freedom is very crucial after deliverance because devil never want to let go of anyone, the temptation will be tense after deliverance and if you are not closer to God you might go back.

You must stand fast in God to maintain your deliverance.

Galatians 5:1

1 Stand fast therefore in the liberty wherewith HaMashiach hath made us free, and be not entangled again with the yoke of bondage.

To maintain your freedom, you must.

1 AVOID SIN

We are not qualified to be saved but we are saved by grace and grace will stop when we continue to sin, and devil know this very well too.

Romans 6:1-2

1 What shall we say then? Shall we continue in sin, that grace may abound?

2 God forbid. How shall we, that are dead to sin, live any longer therein?

And if care is not taking, we might get to the level of sinning willingly which is very dangerous because that is killing Yeshua the second time and we might not be able to come back.

Hebrews 10:26-31

26 For if we sin wilfully after that we have received the knowledge of the truth, there remaineth no more sacrifice for sins,

27 But a certain fearful looking for of judgment and fiery indignation, which shall devour the adversaries.

28 He that despised Moses' law died without mercy under two or three witnesses:

29 Of how much sorer punishment, suppose ye, shall he be thought worthy, who hath trodden under foot the Son of God, and hath counted the blood of the covenant, wherewith he was sanctified, an unholy thing, and hath done despite unto the Spirit of grace?

30 For we know him that hath said, Vengeance belongeth unto me, I will recompense, saith the Lord. And again, The Lord shall judge his people.

31 It is a fearful thing to fall into the hands of the living God.

According to Yeshua when a man goes back to sin after deliverance his latter end will be worst because he will get more demons.

Matthew 12:43-45

43 When the unclean spirit is gone out of a man, he walketh through dry places, seeking rest, and findeth none.

44 Then he saith, I will return into my house from whence I came out; and when he is come, he findeth it empty, swept, and garnished.

45 Then goeth he, and taketh with himself seven other spirits more wicked than himself, and they enter in and dwell there: and the last state of that man is worse than the first. Even so shall it be also unto this wicked generation.

The primary deliverance is deliverance from sins. Yeshua came to save us from sins, all forms of unrighteousness are sins.

Matthew 1:21

21 And she shall bring forth a son, and thou shalt call his name Jesus: for he shall save his people from their sins.

Sins makes him helpless, and devil know this very well so he will do his best to keep you in sin. Satan will put his rod in your lots so you will sin.

Psalm 125:3

3 For the rod of the wicked shall not rest upon the lot of the righteous; lest the righteous put forth their hands unto iniquity.

These rods include, temptation, enticement, seduction, afflictions, persecution, and many more like that.

Yeshua's regular advice after deliverance is "go and sin no more",
Go and sin no more.

John 8:11

11 She said, No man, Lord. And Jesus said unto her, Neither do I condemn thee: go, and sin no more.

Sin no more.

John 5:14

14 Afterward Jesus findeth him in the temple, and said unto him, Behold, thou art made whole: sin no more, lest a worse thing come unto thee.

Live a righteous life and you will be exalted.

Proverbs 14:34

34 Righteousness exalteth a nation: but sin is a reproach to any people.

2 KEEP OUT FEAR

Fear open door to all other spirits. Fear is the opposite of FAITH and our faith in the Lord is our believe in everything the Lord has done, our believe in everything the Lord is doing and our believe in everything he will do.

Fear keeps us in perpetual mental and spiritual bondage.

Hebrews 2:15

15 And deliver them who through fear of death were all their lifetime subject to bondage.

The enemies' feeds on our fear, fear is used to control our mind.

Only you can keep yourself free from mental bondage by not being afraid and refuse to conform but be transformed by the power of God in you.

You must refuse to be what Satan want you to be and be the person you are created to be by feeding your mind in the truth.

Romans 12:2

2 And be not conformed to this world: but be ye transformed by the renewing of your mind, that ye may prove what is that good, and acceptable, and perfect, will of God.

Always remind yourself using this scripture that God has not given you the spirit of fear but of faith.

2 Timothy 1:7

7 For God hath not given us the spirit of fear; but of power, and of love, and of a sound mind.

Fear will come, temptation will come but in the face of this, seek him first and like Yeshua submit your will to him, pray the prayer of submission and you will be surprised at his response.

Satan was there at the garden of gethsemane try to mind controlled Yeshua and put fear in his heart to ask for alternative way to do this rather than go through the shame and the pain of the cross. Thank God Yeshua submitted his will to God.

Matthew 26:39

39 And he went a little farther, and fell on his face, and prayed, saying, O my Father, if it be possible, let this cup pass from me: nevertheless not as I will, but as thou wilt.

And God responded with angels of strength, to strengthens Yeshua.

Luke 22:43

43 And there appeared an angel unto him from heaven, strengthening him.

3 HAVE FAITH AND DOUBT NOT

Hebrews 11:1

1 Now faith is the substance of things hoped for, the evidence of things not seen.

Faith as discussed in the earlier chapter, is the only way to please God, to keep your deliverance and get more deliverance from God.

Hebrews 11:6

6 But without faith it is impossible to please him: for he that cometh to God must believe that he is, and that he is a rewarder of them that diligently seek him.

Doubt is the food and strength of fear, when you begin to doubt God, you begin to weaken the strength of God in you, and you lose your miracles.

According to Yeshua you can only receive what you believe and thus the saying "if you believe it, you can achieve it".

Mark 11:24

24 Therefore I say unto you, What things soever ye desire, when ye pray, believe that ye receive them, and ye shall have them.

If you believe and doubt not, you will move mountains.

Matthew 21:21

21 Yeshua answered and said unto them, Verily I say unto you, If ye have faith, and doubt not, ye shall not only do this which is done to the fig tree, but also if ye shall say unto this mountain, Be thou removed, and be thou cast into the sea; it shall be done.

Doubt divide and weakens the full strength of your mind and will not allow God to have full control over your mind.

James 1:6-8

6 But let him ask in faith, nothing wavering. For he that wavereth is like a wave of the sea driven with the wind and tossed.

7 For let not that man think that he shall receive any thing of the Lord.

8 A double minded man is unstable in all his ways.

Don't pray and fast in fear but do it in faith. Have faith and doubt not.

4 TESTIFY ABOUT HIS GOODNESS

Testimony is a public recounting of our encounter or experience with Yeshua HaMashiach.

Testimony is not speaking about what God does in your life only but is speaking about what he can do also.

Testimony builds our faith and the faith of others both believers and non-believers.

1 Thessalonians 5:11

11 Wherefore comfort yourselves together, and edify one another, even as also ye do.

David said I will tell of your good works.

Psalm 9:1

1 I will praise thee, O Lord, with my whole heart; I will shew forth all thy marvellous works.

You can testify about Yeshua by publishing the word of God or among your family.

Luke 8:39

39 Return to thine own house, and shew how great things God hath done unto thee. And he went his way, and published throughout the whole city how great things Jesus had done unto him.

When you are testifying about Yeshua you are showing that you are not ashamed of him and in return, he acknowledges you before God in the day of trouble.

Matthew 10:32

32 Whosoever therefore shall confess me before men, him will I confess also before my Father which is in heaven.

When you are ashamed to talk about him, he will deny you in the presence of his father.

Luke 9:26

26 For whosoever shall be ashamed of me and of my words, of him shall the Son of man be ashamed, when he shall come in his own glory, and in his Father's, and of the holy angels.

Holy Spirit is assigned to empower you and help you to witness, pray for the power of the Holy Ghost.

Acts 1:8

8 But ye shall receive power, after that the Holy Ghost is come upon you: and ye shall be witnesses unto me both in Jerusalem, and in all Judaea, and in Samaria, and unto the uttermost part of the earth.

Prayers:

Father, empower me to remain in faith even in adverse situation in the name of Yeshua.

Father, I have no power of my own help me in any temptation in the name of Yeshua.

CONCLUSION

God is still in the business of deliverance for his children so they can see the light and know the truth.

For it is the truth that can get you the complete deliverance you need.

John 8:32

32 And ye shall know the truth, and the truth shall make you free.

Know the truth about Yeshua and know the lies about Satan and his devices so that he will not take advantage of you.

2 Corinthians 2:11

11 Lest Satan should get an advantage of us: for we are not ignorant of his devices.

Know that Satan want to keep you at all costs.

By distraction so you don't have full focused on God.

By division both in races and family, he will even go all the way to prevent marriage from happening among believers.

He wants believers to be hypocrites. He wants you to profess your faith in Yeshua with your mouth, but for your actions to contradict what you profess.

The devil wants you to be afraid so he can control you.

The devil wants it all, he wants your worship.

You must submit yourself unto God and resist the devil.

James 4:7

7 Submit yourselves therefore to God. Resist the devil, and he will flee from you.

Resist him in the power and strength of the Lord, pray without ceasing, be sober and be vigilant and endure affliction.

Maintain your deliverance, hold fast to Yeshua he will soon arrive, so another will not take your place.

Revelation 3:11

11 Behold, I come quickly: hold that fast which thou hast, that no man take thy crown.

APPENDIX PRAYER
PERSONAL DELIVERANCE PRAYERS.
Scripture Confession:
Confess the following deliverance scriptures, you can add your own relevance scriptures.

Isaiah 49:24-26
24 Shall the prey be taken from the mighty, or the lawful captive delivered?

25 But thus saith the Lord, Even the captives of the mighty shall be taken away, and the prey of the terrible shall be delivered: for I will contend with him that contendeth with thee, and I will save thy children.

26 And I will feed them that oppress thee with their own flesh; and they shall be drunken with their own blood, as with sweet wine: and all flesh shall know that I the Lord am thy Saviour and thy Redeemer, the mighty One of Jacob.

2 Timothy 4:18
18 And the Lord shall deliver me from every evil work, and will preserve me unto his heavenly kingdom: to whom be glory for ever and ever. Amen.

Galatians 3:13-14
13 Christ hath redeemed us from the curse of the law, being made a curse for us: for it is written, Cursed is every one that hangeth on a tree:

14 That the blessing of Abraham might come on the Gentiles through Yeshua Christ; that we might receive the promise of the Spirit through faith.

Galatians 5:1
1 Stand fast therefore in the liberty wherewith Christ hath made us free, and be not entangled again with the yoke of bondage.
PRAISE & WORSHIP (5-10 minutes)

Use any relevant praise and worship song to saturate you and your environment.

Prayer:

Father, I thank you for this moment of deliverance, I thank you for you will never fail me, I thank you for sustaining me till this moment. I cover this environment with the blood of Yeshua.

I cover my spirit, soul and body, my mind, will and emotion, my senses, my bodily organ and element, my bodily system, my aura and energy system with the blood of Yeshua.

I ask Holy Spirit to take absolute control of everything in the name of Yeshua.

I take authority over satanic atmospheres created by cultic activity, destiny altering images, incantations, ill spoken words, witchcrafts in the name of Yeshua.

I take authority and I change this atmosphere to godly atmosphere; I command the spiritual climate to shift, physical climate to shift and I say let there be light in the name of Yeshua.

I command that this atmosphere must be filled with the Glory of God. Father fills the atmosphere, fills the environment with Your Glory.

I alter this environment and declare it is now suitable for my prayers to thrive, the will of God to thrive and I establish a supernatural environment for deliverance to occur in the name of Yeshua.

STEP ONE

1 Confession and repentance

1 John 1:9

9 If we confess our sins, he is faithful and just to forgive us our sins, and to cleanse us from all unrighteousness.

Leviticus 26:40-42

40 If they shall confess their iniquity, and the iniquity of their fathers, with their trespass which they trespassed against me, and that also they have walked contrary unto me;

41 And that I also have walked contrary unto them, and have brought them into the land of their enemies; if then their uncircumcised hearts be humbled, and they then accept of the punishment of their iniquity:

42 Then will I remember my covenant with Jacob, and also my covenant with Isaac, and also my covenant with Abraham will I remember; and I will remember the land.

I Confess and repent of my sins, sins of my parents, sins of my generation, and the sins of my ancestors in the name of Yeshua.

I repent of the sins of idolatry, Witchcrafts, hatred, murder, abortion, cheating, stealing, adultery, fornication, uncleanness, drunkenness, child molestation, incense, oppression, sodomy, raveling, pride, lie, falsification, and other sins I have committed knowingly or unknowingly in the name of Yeshua.

Father in your mercy withdraw every legal ground of Satan and his agents have to attack me in the name of Yeshua.

2 Genuinely forgive those who offended you.

Mark 11:25

25 And when ye stand praying, forgive, if ye have ought against any: that your Father also which is in heaven may forgive you your trespasses.

Father in the name of Yeshua I forgive everyone that have sin against me in one way or the other. I live them in your hand in the name of Yeshua.

STEP TWO

Break all covenants:

Zechariah 9:11

11 As for thee also, by the blood of thy covenant I have sent forth thy prisoners out of the pit wherein is no water.

There are lots of covenants to break ranging from ancestral, blood to cosmic energy, they are different with individuals. This is just a pattern. As God keep opening your eyes, you keep breaking them.

Prayers:

I break and lose myself from every evil covenant operating in my life in the name of Yeshua.

I break and lose myself from every evil covenant I enter into knowingly or unknowingly in the name of Yeshua.

I break and lose myself from every evil covenant enter into by anyone on my behalf knowingly or unknowingly in the name of Yeshua.

Also, remember to break the covenant of your enemies too, they have covenant with Satan, with death and hell and they have that protect them. Break them.

Isaiah 28:18

18 And your covenant with death shall be disannulled, and your agreement with hell shall not stand; when the overflowing scourge shall pass through, then ye shall be trodden down by it.

Prayers:

I break covenant backing up my enemies in the name of Yeshua.

I break all covenant backing up the battle I am fighting in the name of Yeshua.

(Get the prayer book on breaking all curses and covenant)

Break all curses:

Galatians 3:13-14

13 Christ hath redeemed us from the curse of the law, being made a curse for us: for it is written, Cursed is every one that hangeth on a tree:

14 That the blessing of Abraham might come on the Gentiles through Yeshua Christ; that we might receive the promise of the Spirit through faith.

Just like covenant there are several curses to break too. Ranging from Biblical curses, ancestral, foundational, generation to personal curses. Different with individual.

Curses and covenant are what give demons legal ground to operate in our lives. They are the spirit behind every covenant and curses.

(Get the prayer book on breaking all curses and covenant)

Prayers:

I break and redeem my life from personal curses, parental curses, generational curses, foundational curses, and ancestral curses in the name of Yeshua.

I break and redeem my life from any curses operating in my life by the blood of Yeshua in the name of Yeshua.

STEP THREE

Claim your blessings.

Galatians 3:14

14 That the blessing of Abraham might come on the Gentiles through Yeshua Christ; that we might receive the promise of the Spirit through faith.

Prayers:

I declare and decree that I am blessed in the name of Yeshua.

I am blessed and it cannot be reverse in the name of Yeshua.

I claim the blessing of Abraham, I claim all lost generational blessings all the way to Adam and Eve in the name of Yeshua.

STEP FOUR

Pull down altars.

Altars is the authentic spiritual portals, gate or access to the spiritual realm, it is a place where divine and human world meet.

Effective evil sacrifices and rituals are done at the altars, information, and instructions to demons against believers are carried out from the altars.

Altars opens your and closes your spiritual doors. There are several altars to be destroyed in our lives.

(Get the prayer book on breaking all curses and covenant)

Prayers:

I raise an altar with blood of Yeshua, and I pull down every altar raise against me in the heaven, on earth, in the water, in my father's house, in my mother's house, in my place of birth, in my environment, in my place of work in the name of Yeshua.

Every priest making sacrifices against me in any altar, fall down and die with the altar in the name of Yeshua.

Blood of Yeshua cancel every blood sacrifice speaking against me in the name Yeshua.

STEP FIVE

Renunciation:

Father in the name of Yeshua I renounce, break and loose myself from all forms of witchcrafts, familiar spirits, marine spirits, spirit spouses, ancestral spirits, all occults, death and hell, evil dedication, and initiations in the name of Yeshua.

I renounce, break and loose myself from all other religions, especially Roman Catholicism, Hinduism, Islam, Idolatry, Christianity, and other religions in the name of Yeshua.

I renounce, break and loose myself from all demonic subjection to any man or woman spirits living or dead, birds' spirits, animal spirits, reptilian spirits, animate or inanimate objects in the name of Yeshua.

I renounce pride, rebellion, disobedience, stubbornness, and self-centeredness. I also renounce unbelief, doubt, lies, fear, hatred, and anger in the name of Yeshua.

STEP SIX

Break soul ties and soul contracts.

There are many soul ties to break write then down as you remember and break them.

Father, I break and renounce all evil and ungodly soul ties that I have ever had with forces of darkness (witchcrafts, ex-sexual partners, associates, and other forms of religions) in the name of Yeshua. I cancel any soul contracts ever form with any entities past present and future in the name of Yeshua.

STEP SEVEN

Saturate yourself again in the blood of Yeshua by saying:

I soak my Spirit, soul, and body in the blood of Yeshua seven times.

Lay your hand on your head and the other hand on your belly button and pray like this:

Holy Ghost fire burn from the top of my head to the sole of my feet. Begin to mention every organ of your body by saying: Holy Ghost Fire burn on every organ of my body.

Repeat this seven times:

I drink the blood of Yeshua; I swallow the fire of the Holy Ghost.

STEP EIGHT

Bind and cast out related spirits.

Matthew 18:18

18 Verily I say unto you, Whatsoever ye shall bind on earth shall be bound in heaven: and whatsoever ye shall loose on earth shall be loosed in heaven.

Mark 16:17

17 And these signs shall follow them that believe; In my name shall they cast out devils; they shall speak with new tongues;

Through the blood of Yeshua, I am redeemed out of the hand of the devil and all my sins are forgiven. I hold the blood of Yeshua against you Satan. I belong to Yeshua now spirit, soul, and body.

Satan has no more power over me, no more place inside of me. I renounce all evil spirits completely and declare them to be my enemies.

I bind strong demons, prince of the power of the air, principalities, powers, rulers of darkness of this world and spiritual wickedness in high places in the name of Yeshua.

I bind spirit of death and hell, I bind witchcrafts, marine spirits, familiar spirits, elemental spirits, serpentine spirits, reptilian spirits, Beelzebub, birds and animal spirits in the name of Yeshua.

Yeshua said: "And these signs shall follow them that believe: In my name shall they cast out devils: ...." (Mark 16:17).

I am a believer, and in the name of Yeshua HaMashiach, I exercise my authority and expel all evil spirits. I command them to leave, according to the Word of God and in the name of Yeshua. Amen.

I ask for legions upon legions of angels from heaven in the name of Yeshua to war on my behalf in the name of Yeshua.

Father in heaven, please send your Holy Spirit to fill me up in the name of Yeshua.

Keep quiet: then take a deep breath and breathe out (repeat about 7 times).

STEP NINE

Ask again for the Holy Spirit to fill you anew and afresh.

Seal yourself with the blood of Yeshua and with the fire of the Holy Ghost.

Breath in and exhale and breath in and exhale again as you are saying I breathe in the blood of Yeshua; I breathe in the fire of the Holy Ghost as long as you wish.

Close with praise and worship songs

Remember deliverance is a process. To fully attain your deliverance and possess your possession you must do this several times, days, months, and years. We are to pray without ceasing.

m justified by the mercy of God, and I am saved from every wrath in the name of Yeshua.

REFERENCES:

Unless otherwise noted, all Scripture quotations are from the King James Version of the Bible.

Holy Bible.

https://languages.oup.com/google-dictionary-en/

About the Author

ABOUT THE AUTHOR: Joshua Olumoye is the founder and Pastor of Harmony Heavenly Church a fellowship of genuine believers of Yeshua HaMashiach. He authored more than twenty books, including ***For his glory, Far superior host, Far superior weapons,*** and the best-selling books ***Russia and China leads in end time.*** With the ability to rightly dividing the word through grace of God, he easily brings out the truth of the mystery of the bible.

Milton Keynes UK
Ingram Content Group UK Ltd.
UKHW011938010124
435297UK00001B/112